AND ALL FOR WHAT?

AND ALL FOR WHAT?

D.W.J.Cuddeford

2004 N&M Press reprint (original pub 1933). SB. 226pp

8137   €17 $17   £11.50

Despite a somewhat cynical title I rate this high on the 'richter' scale of Great War memoirs, it is very good, full of incident with some wonderfully descriptive writing. The author, a Glaswegian, was in Nigeria when war broke out and joined a local volunteer force called 'the Nigerian Land Contingent, but he returned to the UK in early 1915, enlisted in the Scots Guards and after fourteen weeks recruit training at the Guards Depot at Caterham he was posted to the 3rd (Reserve) Battalion at Wellington Barracks. The opening few chapters give a lively account of life in the Guards - guard mounting, royal duties and one occasion on Christmas Eve, 1915, when the sergeant of the guard became paralytic and had to be put to bed, but "not before he had staggered out into the middle of Birdcage Walk and challenged anybody in the world to fight!" In January 1916 Cuddeford was commissioned into the HLI and after a spell with the 13th (Reserve) Battalion joined the 12th Battalion in France (46th Brigade, 15th Scottish Division) in August 1916.

His descriptions of life in and out of the trenches make wonderful reading, but two incidents in particular stand out in my mind. The first was in the Battle of Flers-Courcelette in September 1916 at Martinpuich. A sunken road leads from the village to Courcelette, still very visible and probably changed little since 1916. Here Cuddeford, bringing up the ammunition describes seeing what I expect was a record collection of dead and nearly dead Boches. The lane ....was covered with dead and wounded Germans; not just scattered here and there, but literally in heaps.....It stays in my mind because I have been along that road many times and tried to conjure up the scene. And the other occasion was at Monchy le Preux where, following that disastrous cavalry charge by 8th Cavalry Brigade on 11 April 1917 during the Arras offensive, he describes the death of Brig-Gen Bulkeley-Johnson, brigade commanmder, shot in the face by a sniper. Cuddeford's service on the Western Front lasted just a year; at the end of July 1917, before Third Ypres, he was posted to the King's African Rifles and spent the final year of the war in E Africa. Highly commended

AND ALL FOR WHAT?

Some War Time Experiences

BY

D. W. J. CUDDEFORD

HEATH CRANTON LIMITED
6 FLEET LANE LONDON E.C. 4
1933

Printed and bound by Antony Rowe Ltd, Eastbourne

CONTENTS

CHAPTER I

EARLY WAR DAYS IN NIGERIA

THE first news of war I had from a German on the 29th of July 1914. I particularly remember the date because it was my birthday. My German friend and I had been sitting together in the train all the afternoon travelling from Oshogbo to Ibadan, gossiping on every subject except war, and it was only when we were parting that evening that he made the very off-hand remark " Oh, by the way, have you heard that Russia has declared war on Germany ? " He must have got the news earlier in the day from some of his compatriots upline, although we Britishers knew nothing about it at the time. News travelled slower upcountry in Nigeria in those days ; sometimes we got the Reuters' News Telegrams (sent by post from Lagos), and sometimes we didn't.

Events moved quickly during the next few days. All business was thrown out of joint, and we were left in a state of bewilderment by the rapid succession of conflicting rumours that reached us. Some little real information we did get from our respective headquarters at Lagos, but by far the most interesting, and certainly the most exciting news was that passed on to us by word of mouth by those " men in the know " who came up from Lagos, and who themselves had just got it in the Club there straight from the Horse's mouth as it were. One day we heard that the German High Seas Fleet had been sunk in the Channel with all hands ; again, that half-a-million Russians had taken possession of the situation and were going to see the war through for us within a few weeks at the most, and so forth. In fact, according to those early optimistic rumours we were winning the war hands down.

The first real move made by the Government in our district was when they enrolled all eligible Britishers into a volunteer force, the body which was afterwards called the Nigerian Land Contingent. At first they told us we were " Special Constables," but we were just as hopelessly inefficient under that name as any other. Our district Officer, Mr. Grier, jotted our names down in a little scrapbook ; we were issued with ancient Martini-Henri rifles and bayonets, and that, as far as ever I saw, was the whole process of enlistment, except that thenceforth we were expected to turn up for drills clothed in khaki bushshirts and puttees, which, by the way, we had to provide ourselves. Fifteen rounds of ammunition was issued to us, but not the slightest attempt was made at imparting any instruction in musketry and in the use and care of arms. We just took our " guns " home with us and played about with them until we discovered for ourselves how they " opened and shut " and worked generally. The terms we used among ourselves in referring to the parts of our rifles would have thrown a Hythe musketry instructor into a fit ; we would call the muzzle the " spout," and the chamber the " place where you stick the bullet ! " A good while afterwards we were given a little range practice with live ammunition, but on account of our not having had the necessary preliminary instruction in loading, firing position, and so forth, I think it merely had the effect of making several of our members gun-shy. We were all very keen for the first week or two, and very willing to make ourselves as efficient as possible, but our great drawback was lack of instructors. There was one man, a sergeant of the West African Frontier Force—Reid, I think his name was, from whom we did learn a little, but he didn't turn out with us very often, and in any case he was far too good-natured ever to have made a first-class N.C.O. instructor.

In the ordinary way, our own N.C.O.s, who were appointed by the Resident from those among us who had had some experience in the Territorials or the Boy Scouts at home, would come on parade with a copy of Infantry Training in the hand, and this they would study and pore over on the spot, that is, in those intervals when they were not engaged in a hot argument with one or other of us in the ranks as to how some particular movement should be executed.

After a week or two, enthusiasm slackened off. Although we were under strict orders to attend all parades notified by the Resident, unless incapacitated by illness or other cause, and we had all taken an oath to that effect on signing on, the military spirit waned. Some times as many as five enthusiasts would turn up to a parade, which, anyhow, was enough to form fours with, although we were at a loss to know what to do with the odd man out.

Our first real duty came when the big internment camp was formed at Moor Plantation near Ibadan early in September 1914. It rapidly became filled with the Germans arrested in Lagos, also those taken off the German steamers captured and brought into that port, and a little later with Germans captured in the field in Togoland and Cameroons. Our local Germans for some unknown reason were allowed to remain at liberty under a sort of supervision until a later date, but ultimately they were rounded up and interned with the rest. I remember we searched them as they were being passed into the internment camp and relieved them of the liquor which most of them tried to smuggle in, but I don't remember that much of it was '' returned to store.''

For many weeks then onwards, until the prisoners were shipped to England and the internment camp left almost empty, we were called upon to do sentry and guard duty every night from 6 p.m. to 6 a.m., and at that time, when our services really were required, I think we were all pleased and willing to do our little bit, and there was no shirking.

CHAPTER II

I JOIN THE GUARDS

I LANDED at Liverpool by the " Abosso " early in 1915, and on the day following my arrival I presented myself at a recruiting office. My idea then was to join the cavalry, in view of my long experience of horses, but it appeared that all recruiting for cavalry regiments was at the time closed. The officer in charge of the recruiting office was very decent to me, and promised to do what he could towards getting me into the cavalry, though how he was going to do so in face of his own statement that recruiting for that branch of the service was closed I couldn't quite understand. Perhaps if I had had a little more perception at the time I might have become a cavalryman, but if that had come about I don't think I should have had these experiences to write of.

As it was, I proceeded to my home in Glasgow, and after waiting a week in the hope of hearing about the cavalry, I went one morning to the recruiting office in Bath Street and joined the Scots Guards. They put me through a very stiff medical examination before I was accepted, rather an ordeal in fact for one of my modest nature. One might have thought I was aspiring to membership of a Russian ballet, the way they put me though it in a state of nature in that chilly room. However, I passed, and a few days later found me at the Guards Depot at Caterham in Surrey ; the place known to all guardsmen as " Little Sparta."

One of the first questions I was asked there when I reported myself to the sergeant of the guard at the barracks was whether I'd been in the " Force," by which I soon afterwards discovered he meant the police force. That was a question I was often asked during

the first few days. At that time about fifty per cent. of
the Scots Guards reservists were either serving or ex-
policemen, and many a tale I afterwards heard told
among themselves, when they were swapping notes, of
their doings in the "force"; mostly tales of a highly
diverting nature, too. Until then I'd never suspected
that our guardians of the peace were such sports.

I and a few other newly reported recruits were kept
loafing around the barracks for the next few days, until a
sufficient number had arrived to form a new "squad,"
that is, about thirty men. We were a very mixed lot
when collected together, of all sorts and conditions,
including policemen (many), colliers, Clyde shipyard
workers, professional men (including one big clergyman)
and one man who described himself as a "rabbit-catcher."
He was a weird fellow—the rabbit-catcher. I think
professional "poacher" was what he meant, but that
wouldn't have looked well in an official attestation paper.
He was totally illiterate. Afterwards, when we had all
been put into uniform, we gradually lost our individuality
altogether and became merely number so-and-so instead
of owning names of our own. Just tiny cogs in the great
machine, the "amateur" army, which proved too much
for that wonderful German army in the end.

The barracks of the Guards Depot at Caterham are
very large and well laid out. Situated in a beautiful
part of the country, they are, I daresay, perfect models
of what that sort of thing should be. The different
blocks of buildings are each named after a famous general
or battle, and they are intersected by nicely appointed
flower gardens and open grass plots. The parade grounds
are very large and well paved, and there is no lack of
recreation huts and such-like appurtenances, not forgetting that very popular institution the canteen. The
barrack rooms are long and lofty, well lighted and
ventilated. Each contains about forty small folding
iron bedsteads, which during the day are folded up
against the walls to form a sort of chair.

My first impression of an army barrack room was

airiness, I might say chilliness, and astonishing cleanness. The long wooden trestle tables and benches down the centre of the room and the floor were all white as snow, and the other fittings of the room also were absolutely spotless. It was not long before I learned that all this effect was produced by a very little soap, which we had the privilege of purchasing ourselves out of our 1s. 1d. a day, and a tremendous amount of '' elbow-grease,'' also provided by ourselves.

The squad of from thirty to forty men was formed as a distinct unit for training purposes, something on the lines of a platoon, and each squad occupied a barrack room of its own under its own N.C.O. instructor, but in every room there were also two or three '' trained soldiers,'' that is, fully trained guardsmen as distinguished from us recruits; the idea being, I suppose, that this leavening of the old soldier would help to instal the old time-honoured traditions of the British Army into the recruits. If that was the object, I am afraid it was not achieved. We certainly did learn a lot from these old stiffs, but it was mostly in the nature of how best to dodge parades, and '' swinging the lead'' generally. This was not the sort of instruction intended, perhaps, and on the whole I don't think we picked up much worth remembering from the old soldiers. We would maybe have been better without them altogether, when it is borne in mind that at that time most of us had joined up with the intention of becoming proficient and getting to the front in the quickest time possible. In fact, during our training a constant threat held over our heads was that if we didn't smarten up we wouldn't '' get going to the front.''

As for our N.C.O. instructors, I'm quite sure they were the pick of the best type of the old-time foot-guards- man. Many of them had re-enlisted for active service, but had been retained at the depot because they were of more use there than at the front. Most of them, I must say, were the usual foul-mouthed pre-war soldier, but they were the very men for their job, which was to convert recruits in the quickest time possible into well-trained drafts for their regiments. Those of them who had not been to the front rather resented being kept at the depot I think. The first N.C.O. to have charge of our squad was a Corporal Booth, a typical pre-war guardsman of the old school; foul-mouthed and coarse, fairly honest, but a good-hearted and decent fellow for all that. I remember I made rather a *faux pas* the first time we were paraded, shortly after we had been put into uniform. I was passing out of the block when Booth shouted on us to " get fell in." He asked me where I was off to, and I replied that I was just going across to the dry canteen for some cigarettes. He gaped at me open mouthed without a word, whilst I proceeded to the canteen, bought my cigarettes, returned and got " fell in." I heard some time afterwards from another N.C.O. that Cpl. Booth had a lot to say that night over his beer in the Staff N.C.O.s' canteen about the astounding behaviour of a new recruit who held up a parade while he went to buy cigarettes. The thing was quite unheard of, according to his lights.

Cpl. Booth wasn't with us very long. One day a new instructor, a Cpl. Twohig, took over the squad, and we afterwards heard that Booth had been " clinked " overnight for getting drunk. I believed he was reduced to the ranks, but I never saw him again. We were subsequently under Cpl. Twohig throughout the whole of our recruit training, about thirteen weeks altogether, and we couldn't have had a more efficient instructor. Twohig was of much the same type as Booth, in fact, all the N.C.O.s seemed to have been cast in the same mould under the old pre-war Guards system. Some few of them were downright pigs, but I must say that the majority of those with whom I ever had anything to do were quite decent fellows when you got to know them. Reluctance in accepting small tokens of esteem now and then, either in the form of beer or the loan of a shilling or two, was not very noticeable among them, but speaking for myself, I never once bribed an N.C.O., nor did I ever have occasion to complain of ill-treatment or abuse at their hands.

Abuses were not unknown, however. I don't know what the system is now, but at the time I'm speaking of; and that was when the old peacetime methods were still being strictly adhered to; a bad N.C.O. had it in his power to make life a perfect hell for any recruit to whom he took a dislike or had a grudge against. The recruit as a rule had no remedy, as his word would not be taken against an N.C.O.'s. I once saw a sergeant and a corporal of the Irish Guards give a recruit of that regiment a proper dressing down. In that instance, however, the recruit was a real swine of a man, and nobody had any sympathy for him. It was really the best and only way of dealing with such a disgrace to any regiment, with whom all other methods had failed.

CHAPTER III

How Guardsmen were Made

In the Brigade of Guards esprit-de-corps is very strong. Every guardsman, whatever his regiment, is proud of being a guardsman, and there is no regiment to compare with his own. This spirit in recruits is encouraged right from the beginning, and is in fact made part of the training. Every other afternoon for the first few weeks we were lectured by an officer on regimental history, not only of our own regiment, the Scots Guards, but of the whole Guards Brigade. We were required to know all our battle honours by heart, as well as everything else relating to the regiment. In fact, we were taught that we were " IT ! " All this may seem rather useless, and I thought so myself at the time, but I thoroughly believe in it now. After all, infantry training as carried out on modern lines, is all for the purpose of training a body of men to act in cohesion as one compact unit, and without the necessary esprit-de-corps that end is not attained. Early in the war a lot was said and written about the advantage of allowing the private soldier to use his own intelligence, as opposed to the German system of turning out mechanical " cannon-fodder." That theory, if allied to snipers and such like specialists (when acting as such) is all right, but in the main I think that our subsequent dearly-bought experience, especially in the more open warfare of 1917 and 1918, all went to show that the old pre-war training methods were quite sound in principle. As far as I could see, it is only their rigorous and intensive training that makes the Brigade of Guards what they are. Nor did I ever notice that the mechanically trained German ever went out of his way to offer himself up as " cannon-fodder." Later on I served in a regiment in France in which the esprit-de-corps was weak, and I saw the difference. Still later, when I was with the 2nd King's African Rifles, a regiment recruited in the wilds of Nyasaland, I saw esprit-de-corps as strong as ever it was in the Guards, and we fostered it with good results.

Discipline at Caterham was iron, and the training was very stiff. When I joined up I had qualms as to how I would stand the rigorous training and general hardships of military life after my eight years in West Africa. At first I found it very hard indeed ; harder than I ever supposed any work could be, and the discipline was, to say the least, irksome at the beginning. After a week or two, however, I was surprised to find that I could go through the heaviest day without being unduly distressed. At the same time I think I must have shed pounds and pounds of flesh in the form of sweat on that accursed parade ground. It was not always we older men (I was twenty-eight then) who could bear fatigue least. Some of the young chaps, artisans and manual workers who in civil life were accustomed to hard work in the open air, weren't worth a rap in the gymnasium. These boys must lead hard lives nowadays I'm afraid, and ruin their constitutions with " gaspers " and other dissipations.

At Caterham our day started with Reveille at 6 a.m., and from then until five in the afternoon we were kept at it with scarcely a breather. On rising in the morning we first of all folded back our little collapsible beds, with the blankets all folded neatly on top of them ; washed and shaved, and cleaned up our boots, buttons, and a host of other things. Breakfast was at seven, but that didn't take long because there wasn't much of it. From then till the fall-in for parade at 7-45 we dry-scrubbed the floors, wet-scrubbed the tables and benches, polished up the tea cans and washbasins until they were brilliant, cleaned out the washhouse, blackleaded the table-trestles, fireplace, coal-box, etc., and did I don't know how many other little jobs of work, not forgetting a final clean-up for ourselves before going on parade. From being dismissed at 10 until we fell-in again at 10-45 we usually had time for a smoke. Then we were chased up and down the parade ground again till the dismiss at 12 noon for dinner, the real meal of the day. After dinner, as often as not we were detailed for Rations Fatigue, which meant carrying hundredweights of meat, bread, etc., to or from the Quartermaster's Stores. At 1-45 on parade till 3, and again from 3-45 to 5 o'clock. After that we were free for the day.

Wednesdays and Saturdays were half-holidays, but in case we should be pining for something to do on these afternoons, we had to set to immediately after dinner and wet-scrub all the tables and benches, although all that had already been done the same morning, as it was every day. The room orderlies, (known as " swabs ") were appointed daily in rotation, four at a time, and in addition to all the duties already mentioned they had to fetch the food from the cookhouse, clean and wash down the tables after meals, wash up the dishes, etc. They also had to carry all meals to any sport belonging to the squad who happened to be languishing in the guardroom at the time, and generally act as hewers of wood and drawers of water to all the others. I must say though, that any man who had a moment to spare always gave the swabs a hand. These poor swabs on their day at that duty had to turn out to all parades with the rest of the squad. I had several shots at it myself, and I know it's not easy.

Once a week the whole squad was put on to " General Barrack Fatigue," and many a weird job we got. Sometimes it was just plain sweeping up and sluicing down the drains, but once I remember we had to take our dinner knives and scrape the old whitewash off the staircase, preparatory to putting on a fresh coating. Once some other gentlemen and myself were put on to scout around the barrack precincts and pick up odd matches and fag-ends, using the dustbin lids as collecting receptacles. We had got wise by that time though, and we found the best way to show a good bag was to burn a box of matches

B

into the lid. This procedure allowed us more time for a quiet smoke behind the wash-houses. Another time I remember being detailed along with another man to take a dirty and refractory prisoner from the guardroom to the bathhouse and wash him well. We used a scrubbing brush and made a good job of it.

Dinner, as I have said, was the meal of the day, and it was a substantial one. The food, though of course plain, was good and well cooked, and there certainly was plenty of it ; too much in fact for one meal. A great deal of waste went on, because what a man couldn't eat was thrown into the waste bin. I've seen an ordinary farm cart loaded to the brim with scraps of good food from that same waste bin ; consisting entirely of perfectly good meat and vegetables in one huge mass. I believe that wasteful system was changed later on, and well it might be, with so much scarcity among the civil population at home.

Besides dinner we had breakfast, a very scanty one, consisting usually of a basin of tea, a tiny piece of bacon, and a piece of bread rubbed in '' gyppo,'' or bacon fat in the frying pan. All kinds of fat and dripping were known in the army as '' gyppo.'' For tea we had tea (in a basin) and bread and margarine. No one could complain that the food was insufficient, though the manner of dishing it up rather handicapped the man with a fastidious stomach. Plenty of exercise in the open air gave us keen appetites, however, and we used to get very hungry in the late afternoon, but if we wanted any supper we had to buy it ourselves in the coffee-bar. A really satisfying meal could be procured there for a few coppers ; a meal more filling than elegant.

I must not forget a little '' sausage and mashed '' shop near the barracks which did a roaring trade with us. One sausage with some mashed potatoes cost threepence ; ditto with two sausages sixpence. In this local Restaurant de Luxe clients were not provided with knives, and the forks were chained to the table ! The young

ladies who waited on patrons were under strict instructions not to walk out with soldiers !

We did not see much of our officers in the Scots
Guards. At the Depot all parades were under the
Orderly Officer of the day, but as for the company officers
they seemed to take very little to do with the actual
training of the men. That was left almost entirely to the
N.C.O.s, and in fact it is the high quality of the N.C.O.s
that makes the Guards what they are. The N.C.O.s
form the backbone of the whole Guards Brigade. From
what we did see of our officers, with a very few exceptions they all seemed real good sports and keen
soldiers. There was one notable exception, whom we
shall call Capt. " X." I think Cpl. Twohig summed up
the general opinion when he said one day " If that
Capt. ' X ' is what they call a gentleman, I thank God
I'm only a bloody swine ! " Capt. " X " certainly
was far from popular with his men, but most of the
other officers, as far as I could see, were respected and
looked up to.

As I have said, discipline at Caterham was of the
strictest. The most trivial offence or breach of discipline
(imaginary often) was made the occasion for the in-
fliction of a pack-drill or two. Pack-drills were not to
be taken lightly. The criminal sentenced to one paraded
at 5 p.m. in full marching order with the other defaulters,
and for one solid hour he was marched up and down,
backwards and forwards, properly at the slope all the
time. The only respite in the whole hour was a " stand-
at-ease " for five minutes after the first half-hour, and
it was a proper stiff stand-at-ease too, with no standing
easy. I've seen men come off a pack-drill streaming with
perspiration and in the last stage of exhaustion, and I've
done one or two myself and I don't look back on the
experience with glee.

Kit inspections were always an occasion for the en-
forcement of discipline. Once a week we showed kit,
and at those inspections every man's kit had to be laid

out in full; all spread out on properly folded blankets on the floor and in exact order in every detail. This was nominally for the inspection of the company officer, but in reality for the inspection of the Company Segt.-Major who accompanied him. At least, it was always the latter who pulled men up for some delinquency or other, and had pack-drills doled out. Every article of our kit had to be laid out neither an inch to the right nor to the left from where it should be laid according to a chart that hung on the barrackroom wall, and it was not enough to show our spare pair of boots clean—the very soles of the boots had to be polished ! The slightest infringement of these hard and fast rules meant one of the hated pack-drills.

This may seem like carrying things too much to extremes, too Prussian in fact, but I repeat the system was a deliberately thought out one and all for a purpose, that is, the ingraining of habits of obedience in the smallest detail. I don't think it tended to suppress individual initiative, as some people maintain, at least not in those men whose initiative was worth anything ; but rather to teach them to exact obedience from those under them when in time they came to find themselves in control of other men. An army without discipline, or in which every man is allowed to use his own discretion or intelligence in the beginning, would be nothing more than a semi-organised rabble. And many of the recruits I've met sadly needed some disciplining, especially in habits of cleanliness.

After fourteen weeks of the hardest toil I've ever experienced in my life I got through with my recruit training at the Guards Depot, Caterham, and I wasn't sorry.

CHAPTER IV

A Full Blown Guardsman

In September 1915 I was passed up with a draft to the 3rd Battalion Scots Guards at Wellington Barracks, London.

Immediately on arrival at London we were posted to different companies, and for the next twenty days we did nothing but musketry training. For the first ten days the instruction was all on the parade ground, but in the second half of the course we were taken daily by the Tube and District Railway to carry out our firing practice on the range at Rainham in Essex. We used to start every morning very early, and we always got back to Wellington Barracks about 1 o'clock, after which, with the exception of one short parade for the purpose of showing our rifles properly cleaned, we were free for the rest of the day.

On the expiration of our twenty days' musketry course those of us who passed were given one clear week's leave with a free railway warrant. I think most of us passed. They weren't too particular at that time, and I shouldn't wonder but that the butts registers were " cooked " to show good average results for each squad, so as to get them all through and available for drafting to the front in the quickest time possible. At least, there were one or two men in our squad whom we looked upon as hopeless duds, but they seemed to get through the firing test all right. Talking of musketry, I always remember one misty morning on the range at Rainham, when the firing had been particularly bad, and the red flags signalling misses were waving vigorously, one musketry Sergeant-Major, one of the real old crusted type, at length got exasperated and shouted out '' For

God's sake fix bayonets and charge the bloody targets ;
it's your only hope ! "

We now returned from our week's leave as fully
trained soldiers, fit to be called upon for any duty and
available for drafting to the front.   What we liked most
about this new stage of army existence we were entering upon was that we were now '' upsides '' with those old
'' trained soldiers '' who used to lord it over us at Caterham.   By this time we had learnt from experience that
most of what those old depot stiffs used to tell us about
soldiering generally was just so much bilge.   We found
the soldiers we were now among to be of a very different
type ; the real article.   On the other hand, the N.C.Os.
at Wellington Barracks were not nearly so good as the
N.C.Os. at Caterham Depot, for the simple reason, obviously, that the latter were specially selected on account
of their superior ability to act as instructors.

Discipline at Wellington Barracks compared to what
we hitherto had been accustomed to at the Depot was
mild, though probably to the ordinary infantryman of a
line regiment it would seem strict enough.   The hard
course of training at Caterham I suppose had had its
effect, and the habits of obedience and orderliness become
so ingrained that perhaps it was not thought necessary
to keep up to the Spartan standard any longer.   Anyhow,
generally speaking, we had a much easier time, though
when actually on parade we were not allowed to forget
the fact.   There is no doubt that the Caterham training
had a good effect upon a lot of the men.   Some of those
who joined up at the same time as myself, and who at
first had cried aloud to heaven at the bare idea of having
to parade for baths once a week and clean their teeth
every morning, were now almost aggressive in their
cleanliness, and would sneer at Private So-and-so because
he showed a rim on his neck.   There were no regular
bathing parades at Wellington Barracks.   Bathing was
voluntary, and there were plenty of really well fitted up
bathrooms in the basement of each block of buildings

where a hot bath could be had at any time between 11 and 5 daily. They were well patronised too, and one usually had to wait one's turn for a bath. In many ways we were allowed privileges to which we had been strangers before.

As I have said, when we were actually on parade discipline was absolute, but off parade we were allowed to do pretty much as we liked, without being unduly badgered about with fatigues, kit inspections, and so forth. This latitude was not taken advantage of by the men so much as might be thought. Our barrack rooms and kit generally were always kept in first-class order. Though inspections of rooms and kit were rare, when one was held, even a surprise one without warning, everything would be found in order.

Parades at Wellington were easy. We were roused at 6 a.m. by reveille played on the pipes (usually the tune of " Hey Johnny Cope "),and from 6-30 to 7-15 we had a good brisk spell of squad drill, or if it happened to be a cold frosty morning, perhaps a sharp double round the big parade ground. After breakfast the whole battalion fell-in at 9 a.m. for the main parade of the day, which continued till about noon. This parade was the only one attended by all our officers. Usually it took the form of a route march, but sometimes we went to Kensington Gardens for bayonet-fighting practice, or to Hyde Park for company drill. We liked the route marches best. Although we would of course be in full marching order, that is carrying our complete equipment with packs, etc., weighing in all something like fifty pounds, the three hours marching seemed easy for the reason that it took us through the streets of London where there was always plenty to occupy our interest and make us forget to be fatigued. We usually had our pipe-band with us, or else the drums and fifes, and very occasionally the full brass band. The Scots Guards, I may mention, is the only Scottish regiment that marches to the drums and fifes.

How we used to look back on those route marches and

long for the London streets again when later we were on
the terribly monotonous roads in France ; roads always
flanked by horrible rows of elm trees, all of exactly the
same height and planted at exactly the same intervals.
I know of nothing so deadly monotonous and uninterest-
ing as those interminally long and straight state roads of
France.

If we returned to barracks from a route march later
than 12 midday we were free for the remainder of the
day, but if not, we had an hour's " Practice drill " from
2 to 3 p.m. After that, unless a man was a defaulter,
and confined to barracks, he was at liberty to wander out
into London at his own sweet will until 12 midnight, by
which time he was required to be home in bed, otherwise
he ran the risk of losing the privilege for an indefinite
period.

Our own company commander at Wellington Barracks
was Captain Lord Churston, and when out on a route
march, immediately we passed Buckingham Palace;
which of course we always passed marching very correctly
at attention; and had got well round into Constitution
Hill, Lord Churston would give the command to " march
easy " and smoke, always qualifying the latter part of
the order with the remark " If you have got any fags ! "
He himself would then fall out on to the footpath and light
up an ancient pipe he seemed very fond of, and in that
unmilitary fashion he would slouch along by the side of
his company. He was a very unmilitary sort of person
altogether. On the return journey he frequently would
fall out as we were passing Hyde Park Corner and buzz
off to his club in Piccadilly, leaving the second-in-command, Capt. Lord Coke, to march the company back
to barracks and dismiss them.

Lord Churston was always known among the men by
his " maiden name " of Yarde-Buller. We looked
upon him as a terrific sport, and he really was very
popular all round.

CHAPTER V

Royal Guard Mounting

OUR main duty at Wellington Barracks was guard mounting. A man, once he was marked for guard duty, could reckon on being detailed for some guard or other at least once a week. The big guard duties were of course the royal guards at Buckingham and St. James Palaces, and Marlborough House. These were all paraded as one guard. There were other minor guard duties which were paraded and mounted with less ceremony, such as those at Kensington House, Horse Guards Parade (Whitehall), Wellington House, and one over the Powder Magazine in Kensington Gardens. Not many Londoners, I believe, knew of the existence of that powder magazine, but it was a big one and well stocked, mostly underground. The only part of it appearing above ground was a very ordinary-looking squat concrete building. All of these guards were of twenty-four hours duration, and men on coming off guard were exempt from all duty for the twenty-four hours following.

The first " Royal " guard I was detailed for was Buckingham Palace. The parading of this was, and still is, a highly spectacular affair at which the colours are carried, and at the time I am writing of the band always turned out in bearskins and full scarlet uniforms. I remember I was nervous the first time I took part in one. I had a presentiment I was going to do the wrong thing, and sure enough I did, and got " crimed " at the preliminary inspection. My crime was not having my hair clipped short enough at the back, and it cost me one pack-drill when we came off guard.

Later, I began to find guard duty at the royal palaces very interesting, and when I got accustomed to the ceremony, and knew the routine and just what to do, I think I rather enjoyed it. There was so much to see while on sentry go at Buckingham Palace. Emperors and Dukes and such-like exalted personages used to pass in and out all day long, and we had a regular long list of orders posted up inside each sentry box as to whom we should turn out the guard for and present arms to, and so forth. These orders took a lot of swatting up, especially as they differed at the various sentry posts, but if one were in doubt, the policeman on duty, and there were a number of them, always kept one right. The same policemen must have done duty at the palace gates regularly, because they seemed to know the identity of everyone who passed in and out, and what honours were due to each. How would a sentry on duty at the main gates of Buckingham Palace for the first time know that some stout old lady passing out in a taxi-cab was entitled to a salute, unless the policeman kicked twice on the railings or did something else according to the pre-arranged code of signals ? As a matter of fact, on that post we were not supposed to recognise any member of the Royal Family when they passed on foot, and I remember hearing of an elderly Royal Princess, who, when out walking, once pulled up a sentry who presented arms to her and asked him why he was not better acquainted with his orders. Queen Mary when in residence at Buckingham Palace used to pass out almost every day in a pair-horse carriage, very often accompanied by the Princess, and she always looked out and acknowledged the salute with a nod and a smile.

During the night, sentry go was somewhat dull, though up till about 2 or 3 in the morning we used to watch the string of motors returning west from functions in the city, and we often wondered why the deuce we were doing that sort of thing for 1s. 1d. a day while so many people in London were enjoying themselves so utterly regardless of the war. On a bitterly cold night when there were still two hours of dreary sentry go to do before one would be relieved and get a little warmth and rest, we were apt to resent it. However, that would all be forgotten next day.

At St. James Palace the servant girls would sometimes bring us hot coffee during the night, and maybe keep us company for a while. Very irregular, no doubt, but it helped to pass the time. There were some quite nice girls among them too, once you got to know them, and we used to walk them out when off duty. The best way to get to know London is to go about with a London girl, and many a fine afternoon and evening we spent at Richmond or Purley ; not to speak of the Pavilion or the good old Victoria at night. While on this subject I may mention that lots of girls used to come hanging around the barrack gates, and many women too who no doubt looked upon themselves as something superior. They sometimes paid soldiers to take them out !

Another guard duty I rather liked was the one mounted at the Horse Guards Parade, Whitehall. There has always been a mounted guard there from one of the Household Cavalry regiments, which used to be, and still is, one of the sights of London, but in the early part of the war a foot guard was posted there also. The mounted guard was furnished either by the Life Guards from Knightsbridge Barracks or by the Royal Horse Guards, and they always paraded in full uniform ; plumed helmet and cuirass complete, but we clod-hoppers were in khaki of course. The Horse Guards, Whitehall, is a very ancient building, all stone archways and alleys, and narrow wooden stairways. The Provost-Marshal of the British Army, Lord Athlumney, had his office in the same little wooden corridor as our barrack room, and I remember once coming up the narrow stair-way from the kitchen with two plates of stew in either hand (I was orderly man that day) and greasing Lord Athlumney's tunic as he brushed past me. He gave me an accusing sort of look, but said nothing. It was from this little den that he promulgated Court Martial sentences and signed death warrants, and all that sort of thing.

When off duty there we used to go into the cavalry men's room next door and swap notes with them. It is astounding the amount of cleaning and polishing these men had to do. Immediately they came off duty they would start repolishing their helmets and breastplates, belts, buckles, boots, etc. In fact, almost every article they wore seemed to require polishing, even their breeches ! This last may sound strange, but it's a fact. Their riding breeches are made of a sort of white buck-skin leather, and they are cleaned up with a special kind of polishing paste.

When the cavalrymen were through with all their cleaning, we would adjourn with them to the canteen in the basement below and play at " push-'apenny " for pots of beer. The quart seemed to be the normal measure in that canteen. If one didn't want a long drink one asked for a pint, but if no specific quantity was stated a quart would be served as a matter of course. While on duty we were only allowed two quarts of beer per diem, that is, officially.

CHAPTER VI.

LIFE AT WELLINGTON BARRACKS.

COMING off guard, as I have said, we were free for the next twenty-four hours, so we always had plenty of time on our hands, and often we didn't know what to do with ourselves of an evening. We usually made a fairly successful effort to fill in the time, however. Among the friends I made in the regiment were several Londoners, and sometimes they would take me to some weird haunts of theirs. One particular crony of mine lived down in the East End, and with him I often attended the big shows at Wonderland and other centres of the boxing fancy. It was he who first took me to the weekly '' ball '' held in a dancing hall in a street off the Commercial Road. The entrance fee for gentlemen was 1s. (increased price owing to the war !) but ladies were free if accompanied by a gentleman; if not, they weren't allowed in at all. The proceedings at those '' balls '' were remarkably free from ceremony, and as a rule introductions were looked on as quite superfluous. If you saw a likely lady who appeared ownerless you merely went forward and grabbed her. One had to be careful, though. Occasionally you struck a snag, and some truculent gentleman would demand '' 'Oo the 'ell you thought had brought the lidy to the ball and paid 'er ticket ? '' The same gentleman as like as not was leaving the poor girl sitting there all forlorn the whole evening, while he himself was probably having a hilarious time floor-walloping with strange lady partners. All the same, he would be keeping a wary eye on her against trespassers. The ladies didn't seem to mind. In fact they appeared rather to be proud of having someone who took sufficient proprietary interest in them to make a fuss on their account. Occasionally, however, the amenities of the evening would be somewhat marred by a regrettable outburst of feeling among the ladies themselves, but once the combatants were disentangled and the side fights arising therefrom quelled, the ball would proceed as if nothing had happened.

Another bosom friend of mine at that time was Corporal Gator of " Q " Company. The corporal was an old guardsman, and prior to being called up with the Reserve he had been a policeman in Islington. He and I once went down to the cattle show there, and while in his company I think I must have met all the policemen in Islington, both " on-duty " at the show and " off-duty " in the little pubs of the neighbourhood. I remember Cpl Gator another time took me to Islington to see his wife and two little kiddies. They lived in a little back slum, and his wife, poor soul, was trying to make ends meet by working as a post-woman while her husband was on service. They seemed very fond of one another, and it was really quite a nice little home scene until the Corporal, just as we were leaving, spoiled it all by trying to borrow five shillings from Mrs. Gator—without success. The whole alley gleefully hung from their windows to hear what the Corporal and his wife thought of one another ! I didn't go there again.

On other evenings I would go along with different friends to one or other of the big restaurants, or to a night club. A Tommy in khaki at that time was not out of place even in those establishments where evening dress was insisted upon for civilians. London, when one has plenty of spare time on one's hands, is expensive, and I think my monthly expenditure was heavier during the seven months I was a ranker stationed there than later as an officer. My 1s. 1d. a day pay didn't help much.

It was about that time that I was appointed Acting Corporal, a post which carried many onerous duties and much work with it, but no extra pay. I had been selected for promotion before leaving the Depot, but promotions in the ranks were not made too lightly in the Guards Brigade, and a lot of preparation had to be gone through before the selected men were confirmed in their appointments. One of these was a course of " shouting-drill " (i.e., Communicating Practice), and along with several other aspirants to non-commissioned rank I went daily for ten days to a place at Caterham called Hoxton's Field, where we did nothing but drill one another and bawl commands at distances of up to three hundred yards. The immediate effect of this on most of us was that our voices disappeared almost entirely, and we couldn't talk above a whisper for a day or two. However, they soon returned with increased strength, which was further developed by constant practice.

A peculiar thing I observed in the Brigade of Guards was the intense rivalry, amounting almost to animosity, between the different regiments. While we Scots Guards were stationed at Wellington Barracks the Grenadiers were at Chelsea, the Coldstream Guards at Windsor, and the Irish Guards at Esher. It was therefore the Grenadiers we mostly came in contact with, they being the only guards regiment stationed in London besides ourselves.

The boundary between our respective areas, the " no-man's land " as it were, was the region of Victoria Station, and many a disturbance arose in the pubs of that neighbourhood for no other cause than that we belonged to different regiments. As I have already remarked, a large percentage of the men in the Scots Guards were Englishmen, but while in the regiment they seemed to come to look upon themselves as a sort of " naturalised " Scotsmen. Many of them even picked up a Scottish accent, and they always addressed one another as " Jock." The extraordinary thing was that in the rows with the Grenadiers, by far the most patriotic Scotsmen amongst us were our Cockneys. These naturalised Scotsmen were usually the aggressors too, and in their altercations with the Grenadiers (mostly cockneys like themselves) the most weird mixture of dialect would be heard, such as " 'Ere, wot the 'ell dae ye think ye're daein'," or, " Come orf it Cockie, we're no that daft."

On Christmas Eve 1915 I was on duty at the West Gate, Wellington Barracks, as corporal of the guard. It being Christmas time, there were many late comers to barracks that night, but as most of them had taken the precaution to come armed with " hauf mutchkins " (our naturalised Scots could have told you what these were !) we let them pass. The usual strict discipline was relaxed somewhat that evening. Eventually, the sergeant of the guard succumbed to the festive spirit of the season and to repeated nibbles at " hauf mutchkins," and we had to put him to bed, but not before he had staggered out into the middle of Birdcage Walk and challenged anybody in the world to fight !

The result was that I had to perform the sergeant's duties as well as my own, and I was up all night without any sleep changing the sentries and looking out for the Orderly Officer. It was in the early morning, while I was standing outside the guardroom door taking the air preparatory to cleaning up for the relieving of the guard, that news was brought to me (by the regimental tailor) that I had been given a commission in the Highland Light Infantry. In case it may be wondered why the regimental tailor should take a special interest in these matters, I may mention that newly appointed officers usually got their new kit through him. And very good he was at uniforms too.

As soon as the guard was relieved and dismissed I reported at the Orderly Room, and received orders to go on leave pending further instructions from the War Office.

That was my last day with the Scots Guards, and though while with them I knew the hardest times I'd ever up till then experienced in my life, I think I can now look back on the time spent in the ranks with, if not exactly regret, as least the retrospective satisfaction of having gone through with it. While in the Guards I met many good fellows, some of them men of education, and others just real good rough diamonds. For a while afterwards I kept up a desultory sort of correspondence with some of them (often with a 20 franc enclosure for the good of the canteen), but many of them are dead now, and the others I have lost touch with.

CHAPTER VII

AN " OFFICER AND GENTLEMAN."

ON the 4th of January, 1916, I was commissioned as Second-lieutenant in the Highland Light Infantry, and on that date I reported to the Scottish Command School of Instruction at Stirling. The class when assembled numbered about forty newly commissioned officers like myself, representing every Scottish regiment, and all in brand new uniforms and with new kits. We were very self-conscious at first in acknowledging salutes from the men.

Many of the new officers had already done service in the ranks, but quite a large proportion had no service whatever to their credit ; having obtained their commissions direct from the War Office, or else from a cadet school, which is much the same thing.

The course at Stirling lasted six weeks, and included very little parade ground or outdoors work. It dealt mainly with the theoretical side of soldiering, and was just one long series of lectures on organisation and administration, military law and procedure, interior economy, and so forth. Some stress, I may say, was in the beginning laid on etiquette and regimental usage ; or in other words, on how to behave oneself. That part of the instruction I am sorry to say was in one or two cases thrown on stony ground.

In these six short weeks we were rushed through a syllabus embracing a course which could not have been covered in less than eighteen months under the easy-going pre-war system. But then we worked very hard, and though I daresay a good deal of the instruction went in at one ear and out at the other, still a lot of it stuck, and we got a good grounding in the many different subjects. Our Commandant, Major Stead, on opening his lectures used often to say that he worked on the " mud-slinging " principle, that is to say, the harder and faster you throw, the more chance there is of some of it sticking.

Anyhow, it was a pretty strenuous course, and every ounce of work was taken out of us. We started early in the morning and finished at 9 p.m., the only intervals being for meals. Week-end leave, however, was allowed us from 11 a.m. Saturday until 9 a.m. Monday, and I took advantage of every one to run home to Glasgow.

Eventually we passed our final examinations, and with the exception of two duds who were put back for a further course, we were all passed on to our respective battalions.

About the middle of February 1916 I joined my battalion, the 13th Highland Light Infantry, which was then stationed at Catterick, near Richmond, Yorkshire. The day I reported remains a vivid memory. It was a Saturday afternoon, and I walked the five miles from Richmond in a blinding snowstorm, only to be told on arrival that there was no accommodation available in the camp, and that I'd better return and take digs in the hotel at Richmond until the Monday morning. I don't think the adjutant or the quartermaster liked the idea of turning out of their warm tents into the snow and wind merely to find quarters for a new officer, and it was so much easier for them to tell him just to fade off to Richmond for the week-end. However, I was accepted into the fold on the Monday morning, and accommodated in a wooden " hutment " with nine other officers.

I don't think there is much of interest to relate during this period. It was just a continual round of hard work, relieved by an occasional week-end in Darlington or one of the other neighbouring towns. The folks of those towns in the vicinity of the big training camps, seeing us as they did only on those occasions when we came in for amusement, must have been under the impression that we lived an easy life in the army. A visit to the moors during the week would have dispelled that notion at once. As a matter of fact we had none too easy a time, especially when the snow was on the ground, living as we were in draughty wooden huts and tents under more or less service conditions. Wooden huts and tents provide bleak accommodation out on the Yorkshire moors in the depth of winter, and often we sat in mess wearing our greatcoats with the collars turned up. It was a slight foretaste of what we were to experience later in France. However, plenty of hard work is the best tonic in those circumstances, and we got the tonic all right.

At Stirling, as I have said, we had been given a grounding in the theoretical side of the profession, but with the battalion at Catterick our training progressed along with the men's. We were out on all field work with them, and in addition we had to attend many lectures and special classes for officers in the evenings. We didn't do so badly, however, and when the good weather set in it was really fine. One would rise early on a bright spring morning as chirpy as a linnet ; full of the real joy of living.

The 13th Highland Light Infantry, along with the rest of the 12th Reserve Brigade to which it belonged, were moved up north on East Coast defence duty, and in May 1916 I was stationed at Kinross on Loch Leven. Training there continued much as at Catterick, but it was a pleasant change of surroundings for us, especially as it took us back to our own native hills. The weather, too, was very fine all the time we were there.

In June I joined '' C '' Company, which along with Battalion Headquarters was then stationed in the town of Leven on the Firth of Forth. The other companies of the battalion were scattered all over the neighbouring district ; one company being billeted in Haig's distillery at Windygates. It had gone dry, however.

If this is intended to be a record of war experiences, I think I had better cut out the five weeks spent at Leven. It was just one glorious loaf all the time. The company being very much over-officered, there were not enough duties to go round, with the result that we new officers had not nearly sufficient work to keep us employed. Our hardest task consisted in appearing to be busy when the colonel or the adjutant were hovering in the neighbourhood, but we usually managed to keep out of their way. Apart from military duties we had no difficulty whatever in making the time pass, Leven being a very popular seaside resort of the Edinburgh folks in the summer time. The house we were billeted in was right on the esplanade, and in the morning we had only to slip on a burberry and sprint across the sands to the sea. We enjoyed ourselves very much indeed at Leven.

Meanwhile, the big offensive had started on the Somme, and towards the end of July I and several other officers got our marching orders and five days' embarkation leave.

CHAPTER VIII

To France.

EARLY in August 1916 I passed over to France, and after one night spent in Boulogne proceeded to the Base Depot at Etaples, about fourteen miles along the coast. I stayed there just two days, and within less than a week of landing in France I was in the front line right in the thick of it.

The two days I spent at Etaples was an experience, however. On first setting foot in France I was immediately struck by the different military atmosphere. Troops were in evidence everywhere at home at that time certainly, but here in France there was a grim air of stern reality which somehow seemed lacking on the other side of the Channel. Boulogne was full of British troops and military transport of all descriptions, but it was at Etaples that I was first impressed with the immensity of it all. The place was a perfect beehive. It seemed curious to reflect that here at Etaples it was that Buonaparte in 1805 assembled his Grande Armee for the invasion of Britain, a venture which fortunately for us did not come off. Now, a century later, the same old sand dunes as far as the eye could reach were again covered with tents and parks of artillery and transport, but assembled for a very different purpose this time. I have no idea how many troops were in the neighbourhood of Etaples when I was there, but there must have been very many thousands, all waiting to be drafted to the front.

All day long, endless columns of infantry in full marching order passed to and fro between their camps and the various training grounds, sweating in the heat and dust, and marching along silently in quick time with a seriousness and air of determination not to be seen in the troops at home. The general air of efficiency about everything, too, impressed the newcomer, as did the manner in which discipline was kept screwed up to the highest pitch. Military executions were not infrequent at Etaples about that time. It certainly was brought home to one that here at last were the genuine war conditions.

So it was all the time I was in France, as far as my experience went. On going home on leave for the first time, many months later, I was struck by the slackness of the troops at home, but really I don't suppose they were any slacker than when I left. The apparent slackness, no doubt, was merely a matter of contrast with the strict discipline one had become accustomed to see maintained in France.

The whole of my first day at Etaples I was out sweating under full marching order, pack and all, and in the forenoon of the second day I was recalled from the training ground by orders to join immediately the 12th Highland Light Infantry, 15th Scottish Division, on the Somme front. I entrained that same afternoon along with several other officers detailed for the 15th Division, after getting finally fitted out at the Ordnance Stores and drawing two days' emergency rations.

It was a long and tedious railway journey, with many stops and delays, and we didn't reach Amiens until the following afternoon. The same journey could have been accomplished in an hour or two in peace time, but in 1916 all the engines had been run to death and the whole railway system thrown out of joint by the abnormal pressure of military exigencies. On leaving Amiens we crawled on to Albert, which place we reached late in the evening, although it was only a matter of sixteen miles or thereabouts.

Long before we came to Albert it was very evident we were approaching the war area. The market gardens on the swampy banks of the Somme just east of Amiens gave place to open fields still under cultivation, but gradually after a few miles all signs of cultivation disappeared, and the countryside became just so much waste land covered here and there with huge camps consisting of innumerable lines of tents and huts, and long rows of picketed cavalry and artillery horses. This was what we soon came to know as the " back area."

The low grumble of the guns, which we had heard at intervals when the wind was from the east, now became louder as we approached the front, and by the time the train finally crawled to a stop in the wrecked and battered station at Albert the clamour of the big guns in the neighbourhood was deafening. It was dark by then, of course. The train could not have approached Albert in the daylight without being spotted by the German aeroplanes and shelled.

On arrival we heard from a staff transport officer that our battalion was then in the trenches a mile or two in front of the town, but that the battalion transport lines were in the neighbourhood. We sought for the transport officer of our battalion, and after trailing through the more or less ruined streets of the town for the best part of the night and asking innumerable questions of all the soldiers we met, we eventually located him in a broken-down house in the suburbs. Late as it was, he set out a first-class supper of cold meat and pickles for us, for which we were very thankful, having had nothing but dry biscuits and bully-beef since the morning of the day before. He also gave us a tot of whisky, which was the last we had for a while.

That same night, or rather very early in the morning, we were provided with a half-limber to take us and our valises back to the Divisional Detail Camp, until instructions regarding us should be received from our commanding officer. We reached the camp just before dawn and slept on a bank by the roadside until daylight, when we were allocated accommodation in an already overcrowded bell tent.

The 15th Division Detail Camp was at that time situated about midway on the road between Merricourt and Ribemont, not far from the town of Corbie. Most divisions had a detail camp of some sort in the back area. These were formed for the accommodation of details coming up to join the division, such as ourselves, also officers and men who were sent back for a rest, and officers surplus to the trench establishment and kept in reserve to replace casualties at a few hours' notice. There were not many details in the camp when I joined it, and none at all of our own regiment when we arrived. I stopped there two days, and in the afternoon of the second day I proceeded along with another officer named Welsh to join our battalion in the front line.

This officer Welsh was an old friend of mine, we having been together in the 13th Highland Light Infantry. He was always known as " Little Tich," on account of his lack of inches ; he being as small as I am big. Anyhow, Tich and I started off in good fettle, and on reaching the Amiens-Albert road we got a lift on an Army Service Corps G.S. waggon which took us as far as Albert. From there we trudged along the badly cut-up road past Behcourt and through the artillery positions just beyond, where the artillerymen were making the most of the last hour of daylight by blazing away goodo at the Boche positions ; and so on to the ruined village of Contalmaison, which was being badly shelled at the time. There in the darkness we promptly lost ourselves. After a deal of wandering around in the midst of the shelling like a couple of lost sheep, by making enquiries at various dugouts we were eventually provided with an orderly who guided us to the headquarters dugout of our battalion, the 12th Highland Light Infantry. This was in a recently captured German trench near Villa Wood, not very far in front of Contalmaison.

My first experience of a dugout was unfortunate. The steps of this one were very broken up and muddy, and in squeezing my way down I slipped and slithered to the bottom on the small of my back. Rather an undignified entree before my new commanding officer. However, it did not take me very long after that to discover the proper way of getting down into a dugout

in quick time; we soon became adepts at that on the
Somme, which at that time was about the most unhealthy
part of the world.

Immediately on reporting I was detailed to join
'' C '' Company, and that same night, or rather early
morning, found me out with a working party in '' no-
man's land '' digging jumping-off trenches. That was
within a week of my arriving in France.

The 12th Highland Light Infantry belonged to the
46th Infantry Brigade of the 15th Scottish Division
(Maj.-Gen. McCracken), the other two brigades being
the 44th and 45th. It may not be amiss here to give a
cursory sketch of the history of the division.

One of the first divisions formed of the new army,
the 15th, an '' all Scottish '' division, went over to France
early in 1915, and was almost immediately put into the
trenches in the Vermelles sector. There they did good
work in holding the line when that line was a very thin
one, but it was at the battle of Loos on 25th September
1915 that the 15th Division made a great name for themselves, which they always afterwards maintained. I
think I am correct in saying that the 15th was the only
British division in honour of which the French erected
a permanent monument. That monument is at
Bouzancy, but more of that anon.

At the Battle of Loos, that disasterous victory of
which the home papers made so much at the time, the
15th Division not only took part in the capture of the
village of Loos, but advanced far beyond it through the
German positions; not knowing that they were being
left more or less '' in the air '' on account of the attack
to the right and left of them being badly held up by the
Germans. These were the days before offensives were
conducted with prearranged fixed objectives according
to a properly drawn up time table, beyond which no
further advance can be made without orders. The
Germans at Loos soon grasped the situation and counter-
attacked heavily on the flanks of the 15th, which only

managed to extricate itself and retire to an established line after suffering terrible casualties.

After Loos the 15th Division continued to hold the line in that sector, mostly in the neighbourhood of the Hohenzollern Redoubt, at that time a very strong part in the German line. In July 1916 the division was transferred to the Somme front, shortly after the big offensive opened there. On the Somme it was in the 3rd Corps of the 4th Army under General Rawlinson.

The 12th Highland Light Infantry went into the trenches on the Somme early in August, and on the night of the 12th they went over the top for the first time in that sector, against a strong system of trenches known as the Switch Line, in front of the village of Bazentin-le-Petit and a little to the left of the Bois de Foureau ; the " High Wood " of evil memory. That attack failed badly through no fault of the battalion's, and many good lads were left hanging on the German wire that night. A second attack on the same position was made on the 25th, and proved successful.

The battalion was then withdrawn into reserve, but went into the line again early in September, and they remained there until after the second big Battle of the Somme, in which sticky show the 15th took a very creditable part, capturing the village of Martinpuich and out-flanking High Wood, which thereafter was easily occupied.

CHAPTER IX

ON THE SOMME

THE second Battle of the Somme opened on the 15th of September 1916, and is noteworthy as being the first occasion on which tanks were employed against the Germans. Our divisional front before the attack extended roughly from the Albert-Bapume road on our left to High Wood on our right.

For some days before the attack opened we did duty in the front line trenches, or immediately in support to them. The weather was hot for September, and the stench from the unburied bodies scattered all around was perfectly sickening at times, especially in the neighbourhood of High Wood. That place was a shambles. Even now, when the whiff from anything "too dead" reaches me the recollection of High Wood is forcibly brought back to me. Unburied bodies, both British and German, lay tumbled about in all directions in every stage of decomposition. There was no time nor opportunity to bury all the dead in those early days of the Somme offensive, and even far back behind our own lines dead bodies lay rotting in the sun for many weeks after, amidst a litter of broken rifles and equipment, smashed helmets, and all the debris of battle.

While in the trenches before the show, every night we took out working parties into "no-man's" land to construct jumping-off trenches in front of our foremost line. These jumping-off trenches were made for the purpose of providing more accommodation for the additional assault troops that would be brought up to the front line for the next big attack. They could not all have been crushed into the existing trenches with the troops already there without dangerous overcrowding. The Boche seemed fully aware of what we were up to on those nights, and throughout the night he would let off bursts of machine gun fire, and his snipers I think must have worked in relays. We lost several men on that job, but not so many as might be imagined considering the amount of ammunition that was blazed off at us. Night firing is a tricky thing, and even the best marksman is letting off more or less haphazard in the dark, usually much too high. We always had a covering party of skirmishers lying out about fifty yards in front of the working parties to protect them in case of a sudden attack.

On the 13th of September, two days before the big operations started, we were withdrawn to reserve trenches in the neighbourhood of Villa Wood. There we learnt that in the coming attack our battalion would act as reserve to the brigade, but that we would furnish two ammunition carrying parties of twenty men each to go forward with the first wave of the attack and establish ammunition dumps at prearranged points well within the then existing German positions, from which we would keep the front line, as it moved forward, supplied with bombs and S.A.A. as required. I was detailed to take charge of one of these parties, and a Second.-Lieut. McQueen the other.

Most of the day prior to the attack I spent in making a base depot for bombs, etc., in our, then front line, just at the head of a communication trench called High-land Alley. It was a nasty place to get to, a good part of the communicating trench being blown in and exposed to view of the enemy snipers, but we got our arrangements completed by dark. I returned to the company just in time to be informed by the company commander that McQueen and I were required to attend immediately at Brigade Headquarters for final instructions. It was then about 10 o'clock, and the zero hour for the attack was at 4 something in the morning (I forget the exact time). However, McQueen and I trudged down to the Brigade H.Q. dugout at Contalmaison, along a road that was being shelled at the time, and after being kept waiting about for a while we were at last seen by the Staff Captain, who after all had nothing new to add to the instructions we had already received. We got back to our dugout about 1 a.m., very fed-up, with only a couple of hours in which to snatch a little sleep before we started out with our respective parties for the front line.

At 3 a.m. we set out, McQueen up Gordon Alley and I up Highland Alley, and after loading my men at the depot with the supplies they were to carry forward, we moved on in the dark and joined the company forming the first wave of the attack, which was already in position in the front line awaiting the zero hour. These were the 7/8th King's Own Scottish Borderers, forming the right half of the brigade front. On the left were the 10th Scottish Rifles; in support to both these battalions were the 10/11th Highland Light Infantry, and behind these again was our own battalion, the 12th Highland Light Infantry. Our brigade occupied the left of the divisional front, and to the left of the division were the Canadians. I forget what division was on our right, but I think it was the 9th.

It was a weary and nerve trying business lying out there in the dark waiting for zero hour, the time at which the show was billed to start. Everything seemed so very quiet and normal as we lay in no-man's land just before the twilight of dawn. There was nothing to be heard or seen but the peaceful whine of occasional shells passing overhead, and the soft report and brilliant glare of the verey lights which the Germans never ceased to put up from their trenches all night long. It seemed hard to realise that all this was going to be suddenly disturbed within a few minutes by hell let loose.

It was during this fidgety period of waiting that we heard a most extraordinary buzzing and clanking sound coming up from our rear, which puzzled us greatly. We were at a loss to think what it could be, but a little later when dawn broke we saw the cause of it—two tanks—the first we had ever seen. They were both knocked out by German shells that same day, but not before they had done very useful work indeed.

CHAPTER X

BATTLE !

AS the darkness gave way to a wan sort of half light, zero hour arrived and hell was let loose with a vengeance. Our watches had all been synchronised the night before, and on the exact stroke of the second the whole of the 4th British Army, together with the French armies on our right arose and went forward. Simultaneously, the thousands of guns massed behind opened out their barrage. The line of bursting shells jumped forward at the rate of fifty yards a minute, and we, being the first wave of the attack, had to regulate our pace so as to keep just fifty yards behind this barrage, according to the new mode of advance that had been brought into use about that time.

I wonder how many people at home, who in 1916 read in their newspapers all about creeping barrages, realise exactly what advancing under a creeping barrage meant to the leading waves of infantry. Fifty yards is a very short distance to be from a line of bursting shells, whether German or British. If the line of shell fire could possibly have been kept absolutely exact, according to the orders issued by the Staff (who, of course, would not be there !), there would still be plenty of splinters coming back ; but even supposing the artillerymen to be infallible in the gun-laying (which they were not) many guns were worn and inaccurate, and shells fell short.

I don't think I am exaggerating in saying, at least, as far as our own brigade was concerned, that in the early part of the attack quite a third of the very heavy casualties we suffered were caused by our artillery fire. However, the fault did not lie entirely with the artillerymen ; many of our men would persist in pressing on too fast.

In any case, I daresay the system answered the purpose for which it was devised, though it was altered later on.

Fifty yards a minute was our rate of advance, a mere snail's crawl, and as we went on, the men of the first lines of the attack threw forward smoke-producing bombs ('' pea-bombs '') to create a mask of smoke screening the advance. The effect was most weird. A haze of smoke hung over the whole scene ; here and there added to by the black greasy smoke from the heavy howitzer shells which the Germans soon started putting over. It was still not quite light, and as each shell burst the brilliant flash of the explosion lit up the underside of the pall of smoke that hung over everything.

It did not tally in the least with my preconceived notions of a full dress battle. As a boy I was very fond of battle pictures, and I always had an intense admiration for the bewhiskered gentlemen in gay uniforms they depicted careering along on dapple-grey chargers like rocking horses ; all waving encouragement with their swords to one another to get on in front. The enemy too in those pictures always seemed equally well dressed and '' genteel.'' The reality was something very different. A modern artist who aspired to paint a truly realistic picture of a big attack in the dawn on the Somme would not require many colours : grey mostly, for the mud, the sky, the figures, and the landscape generally ; with small dabs of red showing here and there as the light brightened. He might make it more realistic if it were possible to paint in the indescribable racket and uproar; the tearing explosions of shells; the pungent fumes of phosphorous from the high explosives, and the curses and shrieks of mutilated and frightened men. War makes far from a pretty picture in the reality.

We carried the German front positions without much opposition, though with fairly heavy casualties from machine gun fire from beyond, and there I established my first forward ammunition dump in an enemy position shown in our maps as Bacon Trench, after which I

returned with my party to our depot at the head of
Highland Alley for another cargo. I found the dugout in
which we had formed our depot; a sort of big " cubby-
hole " built into the wall of the trench and supported by
timbers, now chock-a-block with wounded men who had
taken refuge there. Also several others suffering more from
acute fright than wounds. The two men I had left on
guard over the depot were quite unable to keep those
people out. However, we pulled them out as quickly and
gently as we could to make working room for ourselves;
but it was only with great difficulty we were able to get
the boxes of S.A.A. and bombs brought out and lifted
up over the top of the trench, on account of the stream
of walking wounded, German as well as our own, which
all the time kept pressing down the narrow trench.
Many of the wounded Germans seemed half demented;
some laughing inanely, others crying; and I noticed more
than one of our own men who had lost their wits and
were shedding tears like children. It is painful to see
full grown men lose their nerve to that degree, but it
seems that the shock of wounds or of seeing wounds inflicted has that effect on some people.

However, I got my carrying party mustered again, and
we set out a second time with supplies for our friends, the
King's Own Scottish Borderers. Although the open
ground was clearer of men by this time; the wounded
and returning parties keeping to the trenches mostly;
the Boche artillery in the meantime had got very busy
and was now shelling our erstwhile front line area very
vigorously, I suppose with the object of preventing our
reinforcements coming up. We had to pass through
this enemy barrage, and I lost six men out of my small
party in doing so. I pushed on this time to a position
just in front of the Factory Line, an intermediate German
system of trenches running from in front of the village
of Martinpuich to the old sugar factory near Courcelette
on the left. Hard fighting was going on in the neighbourhood of Martinpuich when we got there; machine
guns clacking away in every direction. We had a tough

D

job in getting up with our ammunition supplies this time, in fact it was easily the worst trip out of three I made to the front line that day.

The German casualties must have been very heavy. At one part, where the Factory Line crossed a sunken road leading out of Martinpuich, I saw what I expect was a record collection of dead and nearly dead Boches. The bank of this sunken road nearest our lines was honey-combed with dugouts, and evidently the Germans had organised this position as a strong point in their defence. The lane outside the dugouts nearest the trench for a distance of about twenty yards was covered with dead and wounded Germans ; not just scattered here and there, but literally in heaps, so that one could not have counted them without pulling them apart. They had evidently been caught by our shrapnel fire as they came up out of the dugouts. It certainly was a ghastly sight, and though I had already seen a good deal of that sort of thing during the short time I'd been in France, I must confess that for the moment I felt a return of those qualms of horror which I expect everyone, unless he is a butcher by trade, must feel at the beginning.

One could not help feeling surprise at the Germans crowding so many men into such an open position, which would obviously be shelled by our artillery in an attack. I subsequently noticed several times that the Germans seemed to show a decided partiality for sunken roads, the very positions our artillery would be likely to mark down for special attention. These sunken roads, which abound in Picardy and Artois, make admirable defensive positions according to the old code of field defences, but they have the disadvantage nowadays that the enemy is just as well aware of their importance and their exact location as you are, and accordingly concentrates his artillery fire on them. In these days of rapid-fire field howitzers and trench mortars they are too easily marked down, and not worth holding in case of a serious attack. In time, from our own experience, and from noting the effect of our artillery preparation on the Boche positions, we discovered for ourselves this principle of "avoiding the obvious."

For all his heavy casualties that day, and the comparative ease with which we carried his front line system of defences, the Boche here and there put up a very stout resistance, which increased the farther we advanced, as is always the case in these operations. In the Tangle Trench on the outskirts of Martinpuich, I remember seeing a German officer who with his men had apparently made a good hand-to-hand fight of it against the K.O.S.B.s At the time I came up it was all over, and there were eight or nine Germans lying in the trench all bayoneted. The officer himself, though badly wounded in more than one place, judging from the mess he was in, was sitting up in the midst of his men and in quite good English shouting for assistance ; at one moment imploring our boys, and at the next offering money to any of our stretcher bearers who would take him back to a dressing station. One couldn't help feeling sorry for even a German in his plight, but I'm afraid nobody took the slightest notice of him, except to tell him that he could " bloody well wait " until our own wounded had been attended to. Besides, I don't suppose he would have any money left in his pockets by that time, though the poor fellow didn't seem aware of the fact. Our " Jocks " were great at collecting souvenirs ; a man didn't need to be dead before they had cleaned him out.

The third trip I made with ammunition was in the late afternoon to replenish the same dump in the Factory Line. By that time the whole of the village of Martinpuich had been captured and our line established all round the front of it, but bending back on the right to the Star Line (the British name for the front trench of a strong German intermediate system running from Martinpuich to High Wood), and on the left to the road between Martinpuich and Courcelette, which latter village also had been captured by the Canadians. The haul of prisoners from Martinpuich was a very big one, and included the com-

plete staff of a German brigade (what they call a
" Regiment "). The German brigadier himself was a
typical fat and dumpy Hun, and he looked very cross.
The officers of his staff, however, didn't seem to mind so
much, in fact most of them appeared relieved at getting
well out of it.

The prisoners were coming back across the open in big
batches in the late afternoon, often without any escort.
Souvenirs were to be had in plenty ; pickelhaube helmets,
etc. galore, but I don't think we had time to collect many
just then. These things haven't much interest at the
time for people going forward into the thick of it, who are
not sure they will come out of the business with their own
lives much less loaded with souvenirs. By this I am
referring to helmets and suchlike bulky articles. There
was never a " Jock " of the H.L.I., as far as I saw, too
busy to relieve a live, wounded or dead German of such
portable gear as might be worth the taking. Wristlet
watches in particular were cheap in our battalion, and
German paper money was at a discount.

The only thing I had to eat all that day, in fact since
the afternoon of the previous day, was a jam sandwich
given me by a Lieutenant McFarlane of the 10/11th
H.L.I. as we passed over Bacon Trench on our last trip
to the attacking line. Towards dusk, as we were returning, I saw poor McFarlane's body lying just where I
had last spoken to him. I also found that our ammunition dump in Highland Alley had been blown up by a
Boche shell, and the guard I left over it both missing ;
probably blown to bits and buried in the debris. At any
rate we never heard any more of them. The Boche had
certainly got his rag out by this time, and he was giving
our back areas a disgraceful basting with his artillery.

CHAPTER XI

CONSOLIDATING OUR GAINS

ON our return to Highland Alley I was met by an orderly with orders to rejoin the battalion with my party. I found that " C " Company, which with the rest of the battalion had been in reserve all day, had moved up to near our old front line, and were now under orders to move forward to a support position in the Factory Line. We started off in the darkness about 10 p.m. in single file across the open, and though the actual distance we had to cover was only about a mile, we didn't get into our new position until nearly midnight. Making one's way in the darkness across a waste of shell-pitted ground and broken trenches ; through torn-up tangles of barbed wire and other obstacles, is by no means an easy job. The greatest difficulty is in keeping touch with the men in front and behind, and it is only by making frequent halts to allow the people behind to close up that connection can be maintained throughout the column. I was appointed guide to the company that night on account of having already been twice during the day to the place we were now going to, but everything seemed different in the darkness with no landmarks visible, and I confess I felt relieved when at last we reached our destination in the Factory Line.

It was raining hard by then, and bitterly cold. In the section of the trench occupied by my platoon there were no dugouts nor shelters of any kind, so we just had to stand there and get soaked through. There was not even anything to sit upon, and the bottom of the trench was a mass of trampled mud. I had lost my trench coat some days before, but I made the best shift possible with a groundsheet tied around my shoulders with a bit of string. This was what the men usually wore in wet weather. It was not often that greatcoats were taken into the trenches.

Between 1 and 2 a.m. an orderly came up from Battalion H.Q. with a message instructing our company commander, Capt. Miles, to send forward half his company immediately to reinforce the 10/11th H.L.I. in the front line. The platoons detailed for this duty were my own and Welsh's ("Little Tich"), and I was given command of the half-company. The part we were to take over was a section of Gunpit Trench, to the left of the village of Martinpuich, and though I had gained a good idea from our maps of the location of the position we were to get to, we had a terrible job in finding our way there. In the dark we bore too much to the right and found ourselves in the ruined streets of Martinpuich, where we stumbled blindly along over the wreckage of houses which had fallen across the streets. The Boche was shelling the place vigorously all the time, which didn't improve matters for us.

However, just as dawn was breaking, we hit upon the path leading to the left we were looking for, and followed it down to Gunpit Trench.

"Gunpit Trench" wasn't really a trench at all, but part of the sunken road leading from Martinpuich to Courcelette. In the deep end nearest the village the Germans had had a battery of 77 mm field guns ("whizzbangs"), hence the name Gunpit Trench.

This was the part we took over. The Germans had been successful in removing their guns, but the lane was littered with piles of field gun ammunition, both live and empty, also several dead Boche artillerymen. There were a number of defunct infantrymen also lying about in the neighbourhood, all belonging to the 3rd Bavarian Division ; some of Prince Ruprecht's crew.

CHAPTER XII

HOLDING MARTINPUICH

As it grew lighter we could see in front of us the belt of barbed wire marking " Twenty-sixth Avenue," which the Germans were holding in strength. Running diagonally across our half-left, and at no great distance, was the line of trees bordering the Albert-Bapaume road, all still in full leaf and scarcely damaged as yet by artillery fire. The constant crack of rifles from that direction showed that the Boche snipers were taking full advantage of the cover the foliage afforded. The same trees a week or two later were a double row of blasted and blackened stumps.

Some of our aeroplanes were up very early in the morning, and as the result probably of the information they signalled back, our artillery opened the day by giving the enemy a terrific intense bombardment. A continuous stream of shells, mostly eighteen-pounders and howitzers, whistled close over our heads on to the German positions in front for about ten minutes. We could see the high explosives bursting on his trenches and the puffs of shrapnel over his lines, and we hoped the Boche was enjoying himself.

Our own turn was to come a little later. I think our airmen must have spotted a Boche concentration for a counter-attack, because quite early in the morning he opened his artillery on us and followed it up with an infantry attack in full force. We managed to beat them off from our own section of the line, but we could hear the rattle of musketry and the popping of bombs continuing for a little while some few hundred yards to our left. We afterwards heard that some of the Germans had actually got right in among the Canadians on our left, but I don't suppose they got back again. This all happened very early in the day, not so long after dawn, but thereafter things quietened down somewhat for the rest of the morning, and we utilised the time in making fire steps behind the crest of the bank, and constructing shelters of a kind for ourselves down on the roadside.

I must not forget to mention an incident which took place about this time of the day. Our brigadier, Brig-Gen. Matheson of the 46th Brigade, accompanied by his brigade-major, Capt. Horn of the R.S.F., came up to visit the line. Out in front of us there were many wounded lying about among the dead, both German and British, the latter from our attacks of the day before. Gen. Matheson when he heard of it made no more to do but went out over the top, followed by Capt. Horn and one orderly, to see for himself. I thought it a very plucky thing to do, though it certainly seemed somewhat rash in view of the activity of the German snipers, who had already caused us some casualties that morning. The General went back, and a little later sent up a party of German prisoners to collect and bring in the wounded. This small party went out time after time, led by a German warrant officer carrying a red cross flag, and escorted by only two British Tommies. The marvellous thing was that the prisoners made no attempt whatever to bolt for their own lines, though they might easily have done so without much risk. More marvellous still it was to see the two British privates phlegmatically marching along with them, one fore and the other aft of the procession, both appearing as unconcerned as if there wasn't a live German left in the neighbourhood. I must say, to their credit, that the Germans in the opposite trenches made no attempt to molest or fire on this party all the time, though their snipers continued to give us their full attention.

It was during this lull that a warmly welcomed fatigue party managed to make their way to us with rations. The men made a small fire or two under the lee of the road bank, being careful to throw up as little smoke as possible, and one of them cooked me some bacon in his messtin lid, with chunks of bread fried in the fat. The bread had to serve as a plate, but it was one of the most satisfying, though greasy, meals I can ever remember. With the exception of the jam sandwich given me the day before by poor McFarlane I'd had nothing at all to eat for just forty-two hours. This was one of the earliest war lessons I learnt from experience—never to be without some spare rations in these operations. The '' iron rations '' carried as part of their equipment by all troops, officers and men, were never opened except by special order in an emergency.

The same fatigue party brought up a bundle for me from Capt. Miles, our company commander, which on unrolling I found to contain a German officer's ground-sheet and greatcoat. Miles had found them in a dugout. and knowing I was without a coat sent them on to me. It was very cold, and the greatcoat was welcome indeed. Though a bit tight, I wore it for two or three days after, and it was about the smartest coat I have ever sported, being of a french-grey colour with a bright red turndown collar and bronze buttons.

Somewhere about midday the Boche artillery started to get busy again, but this time he set to and subjected us to a long and deliberate bombardment with nasty big black howitzer shells of the kind known to us as '' crumps '' (5.9″ and 8″). It lasted fully an hour, and all that time we could do nothing but sit tight and take what we got. It was evident he knew we were holding the road in force (those sunken roads again), and time after time he placed shells on one bank or the other, and occasionally plumb in the middle of the road. Some-times these would burst with the usual horrible ear-split-ting and tearing explosion of the Boche '' crump '' and when the greasy black smoke had drifted away and you wiped the dirt out of your ears, eyes and mouth, you would perhaps find nothing but a big hole torn in the ground, but nobody hurt. At other times several poor wretches would be left lying on the road, and men wounded by the splinters even at some distance off. Such are the vagaries of shells.

Our casualties were fairly heavy while it lasted, and altogether it was a bad hour ; one of the worst I've experienced. The nerve-trying part of it was that we could do nothing, and we had practically no shelters or protection of any kind. An ordinary trench under heavy shell-fire is bad enough, but it is a far better place to be in during a bombardment than a sunken road.

A little to our right, just where the road cleared the village of Martinpuich, there was a temporary wooden causeway constructed for artillery and wheeled traffic crossing the road from bank to bank. The Boche tried for this with his guns time after time, and eventually a shell struck it fair and square and brought it down. He was not going to leave any of his structures to be used by our people if he could help it.

I think the shock of a severe wound must have the effect of numbing a man's senses at the time. During this bombardment a big shell landed right on the roadway near where we were, killing two men and wounding several others. When the smoke cleared away I happened to be looking at a man sitting on the opposite bank of the road. He was gazing straight in front of him when I first noticed him, but after a second or two he started, whimpered, glanced at his arms, then all over himself, then discovered that the calf of one of his legs, puttee and all, had been carried away by a splinter ! He evidently felt there was something wrong, but didn't quite know where at first.

A little later the Boche left us alone and transferred his attention to other areas. About 4 p.m. orders reached us that we would be relieved by the 8/10th Gordons of the 44th Brigade, which news we were rather pleased to hear. We'd had just about enough of it by that time. In due course, before dark, the Gordons arrived and took over. As the communication trenches leading back were to be kept clear for troops moving into the front line, we received instructions to come back over the top as best we could, so as not to cause congestion in the communication trenches. We accordingly formed up and led off over the open in single file at the double. The column was led by an officer of the 10/11th H.L.I., and we started off as hard as we could, just as the Boche began another attack. He may have thought we were running away, but he would find that our relief, the 8/10th Gordons, were still there waiting for him ; fresh and ready for the fray.

I was in the rear of the column when we doubled away, and with the bullets singing around I must confess I was in a sweat lest I should get one in that part of the anatomy which brave men are not supposed to show to the enemy. I also confess that I didn't by any means feel so '' brave '' then as I did when I went into the show two days before, and I was very glad to be getting out of it for a spell. I suppose it is the effect of no food nor sleep, and the nervous strain ; anyhow, I've always noticed that men go into a show full of beans, but come out after a few days without the same quantity of starch in them.

As a matter of fact, we got back without a single casualty in crossing over the top, which was rather extraordinary, and afterwards we learnt that the Gordons who had come up under cover of the communication trenches had lost heavily in doing so. This is just another instance of the advantage of avoiding the obvious, and doing what the enemy least expect you to do.

We got back to O.G.1 (i.e., Old German Trench No. 1) near Villa Wood, where the battalion was assembled in the old German dugouts in an area now happily a good distance behind our new front line. Our artillery we found had pushed up to beyond this area, and all around were batteries of 18-pounders and field howitzers blazing away good-o at the Boche. That night I had a slap-up feed in our Company dug out, a perfect gorge ! and I slept till midday the next day. It was the first sleep I'd had for three nights, and I badly needed it.

CHAPTER XIII

WE MOVE BACK.

THE next day we remained where we were in reserve, but we had the luxury of a shave and a much needed wash (hands and face only ; we were still in the trenches). The day following we moved a little farther back to dugouts by the roadside between Contalmaison and Bazentin-le-Petit, near to Mametz Wood, and there we stopped one day, still in reserve of course, and expecting to be sent forward again at any moment. The following morning we were finally withdrawn out of the line altogether.

The Battalion made its way back by companies at intervals to Albert, where after a short halt and rest we were joined by our battalion transport. We marched out of Albert, therefore, as a full battalion in column of route with our pipe band at the head. Although we were all pretty well fagged out, I'll never forget the way the men brightened up and stepped out the moment the pipe band struck up. However, the effect didn't last long, for the rain came on, and many men fell out from sheer exhaustion before we reached our destination for the day.

This was Francvilliers, and the billets allotted to us consisted of an open field about half-a-mile from the village. Owing to a blunder somewhere, no tents nor shelters of any kind had been provided for us. The whole battalion was just bivouaced out on the open ground, and there we had to lump it for the night. It was poor comfort for tired men, being housed out in an open stubble field on a bitterly cold and wet Autumn night, with water streaming in torrents across the ground we had to lie on. In the trenches we would at least have had some sort of protection against the biting wind, but here there was not even that. We made the best of a bad job, but it was a drenched and chittering battalion that marched away next morning. However, the morning soon turned out bright and fine, and the sun had put a little more life into us by the time we reached our final destination, where we were to go into rest billets ; a large village called La Housoye, about midway between Albert and Amiens. We marched in in fine fettle, with the pipes playing gayly in front. They had to play without the accompaniment of the drums though, these having got wet and unplayable.

Military pipe music is very fine and stirring, but in my opinion it is the drum combination that makes a pipe band the finest marching music in existence. Without drums there is not the rythm and time essential to military music, the object of which, after all, is to stimulate men to greater marching powers. The Army Council does not provide a band to each battalion just for swank, and so that the men may listen to pretty music. A collection of African tom-toms, so long as they kept proper time, would have a more stimulating effect and serve the purpose better in the long run than the finest Guards band that ever played in London. It is just for this reason that so much importance is attached to "keeping-step" while on the march. Nothing is more tiring than a broken step, that is, with every man pottering along in his own time. When men march in unison, after a while the movement becomes mechanical and fatigue is not felt so much. I know this from my own training in the Guards, with whom the brass band is only used on ceremonial occasions and the drums and fifes on a long route march, and I always think that a battalion of infantry can be fairly accurately judged by noting their step when coming in from a long march. It must never be forgotten that half the strength of an infantry battalion is in its marching powers. The best fighting men in the world are not worth much if they can't transport themselves to the scene of the fighting, and that the infantry have got to do on their own feet. Even in the stagnant trench warfare of 1914/1918 there was a great deal of marching to be done backwards and forwards between the front line and the reserve area behind, and the weight a soldier has to carry about with him nowadays, what with bombs, extra ammunition, entrenching tools, steel helmet, goatskin, or leather jerkin, etc., is much more than the pre-war soldier was expected to carry. Remember also that the pre-war soldier was a picked man of the finest physique, whereas a good number of our '' Jocks '' were men well over active service age who had joined up out of sheer patriotism, though by no means physically fit for the work required of them.

However, I started this paragraph on the subject of pipe bands, but it seems I'm digressing somewhat.

CHAPTER XIV

IN BILLETS AT LA HOUSOYE

ON arrival at La Housoye we got our men housed in the billets allocated to the company, saw them fed and settled down to the work of cleaning themselves and their equipment, which being done we looked around for our own billet. This was in one of the few houses in the village boasting an upper storey, and with the exception of Capt. Miles and a captain of the Trench Mortar Battery, who got a small room between them, our lodging was the landing at the top of the stairs—this for four of us. Our valises were brought up and opened out by our batmen, and the first thing we did was to have a thorough good wash and a complete change. We needed it !

That hot bath, though it was only out of a bucket in the backyard down below (there are no bathrooms in French country houses, at least, not in Picardy, Artois nor Flanders), was perfect bliss. By the time we had made a complete change of clothing and donned clean tunics and tartan trews, we felt ourselves civilised beings once again, and forgot there was such a thing as a war going on a few kilometers away. Just as a person who has never had the toothache can't appreciate the comfort of being without it, neither can those who've never known what it is to be completely and absolutely dirty appreciate the pleasure of being really clean once again.

Our company mess was in the little brick-paved kitchen of a small farmhouse near by, and we were a cheerful gathering at dinner that night. The kitchen was kitchen and living room combined, and the whole of the French family were always there with us when we were at mess ; our cook and Madame using the stove turn about in doing the cooking for their respective families.

They never seem to use ordinary fireplaces in French farmhouses, but always American stoves, and very good ones too.

In the chimney corner behind the stove sat the old Grandpere, an extremely decrepit and ancient person, whom from appearances one might have judged to be about a hundred years old. Old Grandpere sat there daddling a baby all the time, taking not the slightest notice of us. We had managed to get a bottle of whisky that night from H.Q. mess, and we gave Grandpere a small tot. It seemed that Grandpere had served in the Franco-Prussian war, and when at his own urgent request we gave him another tot, Grandpere set down the baby and started to tell us all about what they did to "Les Boches" in 1870 (he didn't say much about what Les Boches did to them !). It ended in Madame leading him gently away to bed, the old boy all the time piping out the Marseillais at the pitch of his poor old squeaky voice.

The next morning I had the pleasure of learning in the Orderly Room that I was being recommended for the Military Cross for good work done in maintaining the supply of ammunition to the firing line during the recent operations. I was of course greatly elated, and received congratulations from the other officers. I'm still waiting for that M.C.

We remained ten days in rest billets at La Housoye, recuperating and getting fitted out again, and during that time we did only the usual practice drilling in the fields of the neighbourhood. In those ten days I managed twice to get into Amiens for the afternoon and evening with some of the other officers, and we had quite a good time there. Except for fairly frequent air-raids, Amiens at that time was almost untouched by war, and I thought it quite worthy of its description as the capital of the north of France. Amiens is a very nice town indeed, quite a lesser Paris in its way, but the people are very mean, and not at all like the Parisians. Our great rendezvous was a little fish shop in a side street, which had a supper room upstairs where you were served with the finest '' langouste '' and the best wine in France. That little place is famous in its way for its lobster suppers, even among the best French people. It is nearly opposite the big American Bar, and although it has a very unprepossessing exterior for a restaurant the place is well known in Amiens, or was at that time.

Shortly before we left La Housoye our commanding officer, Lieut.- Col. Hayman, went sick, and the command of the battalion was taken over by a new commanding officer, Lieut.-Col. the Earl of Rothes.

E

CHAPTER XV

AT ALBERT

We moved back to the front line about the end of September, and it was a very different battalion that marched out of La Housoye from the bedraggled and worn out mob that had trailed themselves in ten days before. Some of the Jocks who had crawled in then bemoaning the day they had ever " j'ined up " were now among the loudest in talking about what the Boche had to expect from them as soon as they got back into his neighbourhood. It was evident we were full of " morale" once again !

At Albert we went into Brigade Reserve in billets in the Rue des Capuchins. There we remained three or four days before we were moved farther forward, and during that time we continued to carry out the usual daily squad drill and physical training on a piece of waste ground just outside the town on the road to Bray-sur-Somme. The houses we were billeted in were all more or less ruined by shell fire, and daily while we were there the German artillery knocked a few more lumps off them. He never omitted to carry out a long range bombardment of Albert each day, and during the night too his shells would come over at intervals. This shelling all seemed to come from the north ; from the direction of Thiepval, which part of the front line at that time was still much too near Albert for comfort.

I remember the day after we got into Albert our battalion H.Q. staff were very dissatisfied with the billet allotted to them, but after some fuss with the Town Major they were given much better quarters in a fine house almost opposite the public baths. The day after they entered into possession of their new billet, the Boche put over a big one that went right through the front of the house and laid out every one of our H.Q. staff who were present at the time. These were the commanding officer (the Earl of Rothes), the second in command (Major Dixon), the adjutant (Capt. Watson), the senior captain (Capt. Shaw), the medical officer (Capt. McGorty) and the padre. It happened just as they had finished lunch, and the wonderful part was that none were killed outright, though all of them were more or less seriously wounded. The Earl of Rothes lost an eye, and it was remarked by one of our socialists (we had a number of these) that his blue blood was just as red as other folk's ! Whatever the colour of his blood, he was a very popular commanding officer, and we were sorry to lose him.

On the same morning, a German shell—one of many—landed just behind our own billet and knocked down part of a high brick wall that surrounded the property. One of the new officers with us who had recently joined the battalion while we were out refitting, Second.-Lieut. McDougall (an Irishman), to whom all this was new, rushed round to view the damage, and he arrived just in time to have the remainder of the wall pushed over on top of him by another shell. We dug him out from the bricks and rubble, and as he sat there waiting for the stretcher bearers, with his bleeding face all covered with brick dust, and telling us all about how it happened in his garrulous Irish way, we simply howled with laughter, as if it were the funniest thing he could have done for our amusement. As I think of it now, there really could have been nothing very funny about it, and I merely mention the incident as showing how perverted our idea of humour had become.

CHAPTER XVI

BACK IN THE TRENCHES

THE brigade went forward from Divisional Reserve into the firing line early in October (1916), and our battalion, after doing a couple of days in Prue Trench, between Martinpuich and High Wood, had a short but busy time at Destremont Farm and Le Sars, after which we came back for a breather to brigade reserve in the same old dugouts on the Contalmaison/Bazentin-le-Petit road.

I scarcely think there would be much interest in recounting this period in detail. It would merely be a record of blood and muck and misery, which is apt to become monotonous. It rained nearly all the time, and the trenches were in an indescribable state. These trenches had all been hastily constructed by the Germans, before we took them over from them, without any attempt whatever at rivetting or duckboarding, and when the October rains set in they mostly collapsed and became nothing more than ditches half filled with semi-liquid and glutinous mud. At night, and sometimes even in the day time, we gave up using the communication trenches altogether, and moved to and from the firing line across the open. Sometimes, on account of the brilliant flares the Germans never ceased to put up all night long, and which turned night into day, we were forced to keep to the communicating trenches in the neighbourhood of the firing line. At those times, men who stumbled and fell into the deep treacle-like mud, or who got stuck and were unable to extricate themselves, ran the danger of being trampled in and smothered by those following behind. That actually happened, and I saw several instances of it myself.

There were many obstacles in those wrecked and more

or less collapsed ditches, and as you waded along knee-deep in mud in the pitch darkness, rendered all the more black in the shadows cast by the brilliant white magnesium flares put up by the Germans, it was often impossible to tell what you were clambering over. More than once on investigation we found that the column had been trampling over one of our own men, or a man of a unit which had recently used the communication trench. By that time the poor devils weren't worth rescuing.

I have mentioned the flares the Germans used at night, the light from which made us keep to the trenches while in the proximity of the front line. We too had our "verey" lights, and pistols for the use of these were normally provided to every platoon in the front line, but all the time I was on the Somme front I never once saw a light put up from our own trenches. Also, we were supposed to have an "S.O.S." code of signals in coloured lights, for use in case of an attack by the enemy, but so far as I can remember we seldom bothered even to learn what the current S.O.S. signal was. Remember that at that time we were the agressors. We rarely put up lights ourselves, and there was no need for it as a rule, because the Boche usually gave us more light than we wanted from his flares, which lighted up the area far behind the actual firing line.

The Germans seemed to be much better at making that sort of illuminations than ourselves; at any rate their lights were far superior to ours, and some of the fire signals they would send up in the night time were very beautiful. Besides the ordinary magnesium flares, which were used solely for the purpose of illuminating the darkness, he had all sorts of fancy and coloured lights. Sometimes you would hear the sort report of a pistol from his trenches, and a light would stream up bursting into a most beautiful shower of golden or silver rain. At other times they would break into red or green balls of fire, or again, a succession of different coloured flares would stream up from his lines.

As may well be imagined, all this pretty pyrotechnical display was not arranged by the Germans merely to keep us amused, and whenever we saw something new going up we wondered what fresh devilry he was up to. Every different coloured light, or combination of lights, conveyed a signal back to his rear ; either an S.O.S. calling for a barrage on us, or to his artillery to lengthen range ; or maybe signalling an infantry " relief complete," and so on. They used a different code of signals on the various army corps fronts, and these again were frequently changed so that we might not get to know the meaning of them. Nevertheless, from the information gathered from prisoners and other sources, our Corps Intelligence was kept pretty well up to date.

I remember just before we went into the trenches on this occasion our Divisional Intelligence Report (known to us as " Comic Cuts ") a secret circular issued by the Divisional H.Q. containing all the information known about the enemy on our own divisional front, mentioned that the Boche S.O.S. at that date was a light breaking into four red balls. We had an opportunity of verifying this information the very first night, for as we were making our way down to the firing line at Le Sars, four red balls burst over the German lines, and within a minute or two the signal was answered by a most hellish barrage from his guns. We had no doubt been observed in the light from his ordinary white flares.

At the same time, the Germans at this stage of the Somme operations repeatedly showed their nervousness by putting up their S.O.S and opening out their barrage without the slightest pretext whatever. There is no doubt but that they were nervy. Although they had brought their very finest divisions to the Somme front, into the "Hell's Kettle" as they themselves named it, their infantry had little morale, as was time after time proved by the easiness with which we captured prisoners. If it had not been for the heavy rains which set in in October 1916, and which rendered all communication and movement well nigh impossible, I really believe we should have had them beaten conclusively there and then on the Somme. At least, that was the general opinion among the infantry, who after all bore the brunt of the actual fighting and should have known most about it.

When the Earl of Rothes was wounded the command of our battalion was taken over temporarily by Major Dennis of the K.O.S.B's (a most popular officer, and a fine soldier), but while we were in the trenches a new commanding officer arrived, who retained command of the battalion from then on until after I left it, but I am afraid, he was never very popular with officers nor men.

CHAPTER XVII

IMPENDING OPERATIONS

As already mentioned, we came back to brigade reserve in trenches and dugouts in the neighbourhood of Contalmaison, and while we were there I was called to the orderly room (a dugout) by the commanding officer, and because of my slight knowledge of German I was selected to do duty with the Divisional Provost Marshal in the collection of prisoners during the forthcoming operations. That was in the second week of October 1916.

It was perhaps not generally known, but I believe it was the case, that a renewed offensive on the Somme on a greater scale than any hitherto, and with co-operative offensives at Arras and elsewhere (of which the operations at Thiepval and on the Ancre were a part), had been planned to take place about that time. If it had materialised under favourable weather conditions, it is probable that the Boche, who then appeared very groggy from the repeated knocks he had suffered on the Somme front, would have received that final knock-out which (*we* thought !) was all that was required at the time to beat him decisively. However, I suppose I am now infringing on matters of high military policy far above the heads of poor ordinary infantrymen, and no doubt there were world-wide considerations influencing that policy of which we could know nothing. We saw and knew only what was happening in our own immediate neighbourhood—that to us was the whole war ! I have dilated on this merely as showing that our morale must have been good—perhaps because we felt that it would be better to get right on with the terrible business and finish it as quickly as possible one way or the other for good and all.

As it was, the continued rains made big movements of troops and transport impossible, and the great offensive was first postponed and then finally abandoned. By the time the next big operations opened at Arras in the spring of 1917, the Germans had recovered from the effects of the Somme attacks.

As regards myself, I reported at Divisional Head-quarters and received all instructions from the A.P.M., an officer of the Coldstream Guards, as to my duties as his assistant. Besides forty infantrymen of my own battalion, I was to have twenty men from the Divisional Squadron under my command. These latter were for the purpose of acting as escorts to the prisoners from Destremont Farm (where I was to receive and " classify " them) to the Corps " cage " which had already been arranged at Bazentin-le-Petit. However, the whole thing fell through, the big operations, as I have said, being postponed and finally abandoned on account of the weather.

My divisional job lasted just one day. All my visions of a staff job with red tabs vanished when I was instructed to rejoin my battalion the day after for ordinary trench duty.

When I rejoined the battalion in the reserve trenches at Contalmaison I found we were under orders to go into the line on the evening of the day following. As it happened, our company commander, Capt. Miles, went sick that day, and at the last minute I was instructed to take command of the company for the time being. It was my first command, and having to take over at such short notice just before going into the firing line, I felt at first a little apprehensive in case things should not go right. However, we did ten days in the front and support trenches about Le Sars without anything untoward happening, and with not too many casualties.

There was only one occurrence worth mentioning during these ten days, and that was that *our own* artillery set to one afternoon and gave us a drubbing. It hap-

pened to the two platoons garrisoning Le Sars South
Trench, a trench running diagonally round the right side
of the village of Le Sars. It was not an intense bombardment, but battery salvoes at intervals of about ten
minutes, all seemingly coming from the same battery,
and there was no doubt from the way the shells landed
that they were deliberately trying for that particular
trench. I sent a message back over the telephone to
Battalion H.Q. informing them of what was happening,
and about forty minutes later I got a reply back from
Divisional Artillery Headquarters enquiring the direction the shells were coming from, as they were unable
to locate the particular battery that evidently had taken
a spite at us. They must have thought we could see the
shells coming through the air, or perhaps that we were
able to take a compass bearing on their line of flight.
All we knew was that they were most decidedly coming
from the wrong direction.

It lasted until after dark, and we never were able to
discover the cause of it. Probably some young artillery
officer, perhaps belonging to another division, had not
kept his trench map up to date (our trench had been in
the hands of the Germans only a short time before),
and was firing off salvoes under the impression that he
was giving the enemy a hell of a time. Anyhow, we had
not a single casualty from this bombardment, though it
knocked the trench about a good deal and caused a lot of
work afterwards in making repairs. Quite half of the
shells I should think were '' duds,'' which whacked into
the mud without exploding. I think that annoyed us
more than anything. If there had been a few casualties
we should at least have had the satisfaction of knowing
what the Boche suffered under our artillery fire. Really,
of course, it was just a matter of luck, and of the rotten
American shells they were using at that time not detonat-
ing on soft ground.

CHAPTER XVIII

OUT AGAIN

WE withdrew in due course to the brigade reserve area in Prue Trench, and there Capt Miles resumed command of the company. The whole battalion, after two days in brigade reserve, were now to go back still farther into divisional reserve, and in the meantime Capt. Hannah of " D " Company, Capt. Johnstone of " A " Company and myself were allowed to go off to Albert for a two days holiday.

Hannah and I ploughed our way back to Albert, and there in our Quartermaster's Stores in the old Rue des Capuchins we sought out our valises ; had a much needed bath out of a tin bucket, changed into clean clothes and tartan trews, and the same afternoon found us in Amiens, where we made an evening of it.

We got back to Albert about 2 a.m. by way of what motor vehicles we could jump on to, and on arrival at our broken down billet in the Q.M. stores I found an urgent message from the Adjutant awaiting me with orders to report at Battalion H.Q. at 10 a.m. that morning. H.Q. being still right up in the line beyond Prue Trench, I had to set to immediately and change once again into my trench rig, and after a very hurried breakfast I started out before daylight for the trenches. I got a lift on an Army Service Corps " G.S." wagon which took me by way of Fricourt and Mametz to the neighbourhood of Bazentin Wood, whence I made my way forward to the trenches on foot. On arrival at H.Q. dugout it turned out that I was required to take back one of our officers under arrest. This was Second.-Lieut. McQueen of " B " Company, the officer who had acted with me in the Martinpuich ammunition supply business on 15th September. McQueen, it seemed had had some trouble with his company commander, which resulted in McQueen being put under arrest for insubordination.

The details of the case have nothing to do with this narrative. In compliance with my orders I disarmed McQueen and took him back with me under arrest to Scott's Wood near Behcourt, there to await the arrival of the battalion, which was coming back to that area the same evening.

McQueen was a very decent fellow, but headstrong and wilful. He and I were intimate friends, but I now found myself in the position of gaoler to him and responsible for his person. He was subsequently tried by Court Martial and got off lightly with a " reprimand," at which we were all very pleased ; the men as well as the officers. McQueen was eventually killed at Arras in April of 1917. He was shot through the head by a German sniper while sprinting for a shell-hole a few yards from where I was lying at the time.

The battalion came out of the trenches that same evening, and after one night spent at Scott's Wood we moved back early the next morning to the village of Millencourt, four or five kilometers to the west of Albert, where we went into billets. My prisoner McQueen and I had a very comfortable little billet to ourselves in a tiny cottage on the outskirts of the village, and during the three days I acted as his escort we filled in the time quite nicely playing " double-demon " patience for one-franc points. In the afternoon I had to take my prisoner out for exercise, and our exercise always led us in the direction of a nearby village where we had discovered a very cosy little estaminet. On the third day at Millencourt the job of escort was taken over from me by Second-Lieut. Welsh (" Little Tich "), and I rejoined the company.

An evening or two after Tich took over the escort duty, as we were sitting around the table after dinner in our Company mess, Tich staggered in, and in very incoherent tones demanded whether we had seen anything of his prisoner. It appeared that the pair of them had

gone out for the usual " exercise " (McQueen had shown
the way !) and it ended in both of them getting " blotto "
and Tich losing his prisoner. However, we soon located
the missing one in the same old estaminet, where he had
been all the time having a hilarious time with madame
and her daughters. We got the pair of them, prisoner
and escort, back to their billet and saw them safely to bed.

After nearly a week at Millencourt the battalion proceeded to Henencourt, a place mentioned by old Sir John
Froissart in his Chronicles as the scene of a famous
fight between the French and English in the fourteenth
century. We only stopped one night at Henencourt, in
huts in a dripping wet wood, and the following day we
moved back to Millencourt once again, and there we
put in four more days.

It was at this time that some German airmen came over
and blew up the big French ammunition dump near
Bray-sur-Somme, It happened about 10 o'clock one
evening. There was a tremendous explosion that shook
the houses in Millencourt like an earthquake. This was
followed by a succession of lesser explosions, punctuated
now and then by terrific thumps that made the earth
tremble and kept every window in the place rattling.
The whole sky to the south was aglow, and the flash
from each fresh explosion as it occurred showed gigantic
pillars of smoke towering up to an immense height.
Our men on the first alarm ran out of their billets thinking
the explosions were taking place a few fields off, but as a
matter of fact, Bray-sur-Somme, where the dump had
gone up, was a matter of many kilometers away. I don't
know how many lives were lost by the French that night,
nor how much money went up in smoke, but one thing
seems fairly certain, and that is that the German airmen
who caused the damage must themselves have been over-
whelmed in the tremendous concussion.

While we were at Millencourt this time (October 1916)
I was given the command of " B " Company. It was
very nice to have a company of my own, of course, but

in a way I was sorry to leave " C " Company, in which I had got to know everyone intimately, from Capt. Miles down to the buglers. I also felt that the taking over of the command was rather resented by the officers of " B " Company, all of whom were my seniors in point of service, though perhaps not in trench warfare. However, they were all very decent fellows, and within a day or two they thawed somewhat and thenceforth everything went swimmingly.

CHAPTER XIX

A Reshuffling

ABOUT the beginning of November we received instructions that the whole division, artillery and all, would move back to army reserve, and shortly afterwards we marched from Millencourt right back to Naours, a village about ten kilometers due north of Amiens. This was a long way back, quite away from the war zone altogether and out of earshot of the guns, and also well off the main routes leading to the front. We did not get there in one march, but were billeted two days en route at Baizioux, where we were accommodated in tents just outside the village. On arrival at Naours we settled down in fairly comfortable billets of the usual farmyard type, and there we remained anchored for about three weeks having a very restful and peaceful time, with nothing in the way of " alarums and excursions " to disturb us, although we were not by any means allowed to idle away the time. From early dawn until four each afternoon we turned out for the good old routine " parade ground " practices, i.e., squad drill, rifle exercises, physical training, etc., of which most of the men really were badly in need at the time. A long spell in the trenches always had a bad effect on the discipline and general efficiency of a battalion, and this unavoidable slackness could only be counteracted by a stiff course of training when we came out for a rest.

The " rest " certainly was more mental than physical, and occasionally you would overhear one Jock querulously complaining to another " Ca' this a rest—it's elephants they want for this job." However, it at least kept them employed, and if they'd had too much time hanging on their hands they would only have got into mischief with the French people. They got into more than enough mischief as it was.

While we were at Naours there was another reshuffling in the battalion organisation, in which I exchanged my recently acquired " B " Company for the appointment of Assistant Adjutant.

This didn't appeal to me at all, especially as I had just got to know my new company sufficiently well to regret losing it, and in any case I much preferred being out on field work with a company to the pettyfogging administrative duties of Assistant Adjutant. However, I didn't hold the assistant post long, because two or three days later the Adjutant, Capt. Russell-Brown, went on four days leave to Paris, on which I temporarily assumed the full duties of adjutant. On his return from Paris Capt. Russell-Brown promptly went sick and was sent home on regular home leave, from which he didn't return until several weeks later. During his absence I acted as adjutant, and though that appointment of course carries many privileges with it, I didn't like it too much.

The duties of an adjutant in France were arduous and never ended. Even while we were out of the line resting at Naours there were shoals of work in connection with re-fitting, rationing, and interior economy generally, and scarcely a night passed without me being roused by messages over the telephone from Brigade Headquarters. A telephone was always rigged up alongside my bed. I didn't mind the work, in fact I found it very interesting, and it gave me a splendid insight into battalion and brigade organisation, but I disliked being cooped up in the orderly room all day and most of the night, instead of being out doing company work, and I particularly disliked having to live and mess with Battalion Headquarters instead of our own little company mess. The whole atmosphere of our H.Q. mess, at any rate while I was with it, was estranged by the universal unpopularity of our new commanding officer, a man who never seemed to get on with anyone.

He came to us from an English Yeomanry regiment, and he had taken over command of the battalion during our last tour in the trenches, but from the day he joined us he was never popular, neither with the officers nor the men. He was one of those people who seem to have the unfortunate knack of always doing the wrong thing and of getting up against everyone they come into contact with, though perhaps acting all the time with the best of intentions. While I acted in the capacity of adjutant to this Colonel, with whom I must say that I, personally, got on very well, I was in the position of knowing that as a rule he certainly did what he genuinely considered to be the correct thing, and once in private he somewhat regretfully remarked to me that whenever he tried to do anyone a good turn his action always seemed to have the opposite result. He was fully aware of his unpopularity, and I really believe no one regretted it more than himself. Nevertheless, I am afraid he was deficient in ordinary tact, and he would impatiently resent any advice, however respectfully offered by officers who knew the men of the battalion—Glasgow men mostly, and miners from the Lanark coalfields—far better than he did. He was an Englishman, and though I don't for a moment suggest that that prejudiced the battalion against him ; we already having several highly respected English officers serving with us ; still, at the same time I maintain that it requires an Englishman of the proper stamp to command a battalion of the Highland Light Infantry, or any other Scottish regiment for that matter. I am afraid our new Colonel did not fill the bill.

I mention all this in detail as showing the difficulties I found in my duties as adjutant and in acting as intermediary between the commanding officer and the battalion, and also as indicating in some measure the influence for good or bad a commanding officer can exert over his battalion. Though the discipline and. efficiency of the 12th Highland Light Infantry was excellent at that time, it was all maintained out of sheer *esprit-de-corps*, and from the same feeling and the efforts of the company officers it was kept up throughout, despite the adverse influence of our unpopular C.O.

F

CHAPTER XX

VILLAGE LIFE AT NAOURS

NAOURS is quite a large village, and a very pleasant sort of place in its way, and like all the other villages and hamlets in that part of the north of France it is comprised mainly of a collection of small farms. With the exception of the country chateaux, which generally are a sort of dilapidated mansion and farm combined, an isolated farmhouse is an uncommon feature of the landscape in those parts. The farms all seem to be huddled up into small villages, and they are mostly very small farms ; quite different from our idea of a farm at home. It might be more correct to say that every villager in France is a small farmer, owning his two or three little fields in the neighbourhood of his village. The fields are all very tiny, and they are never fenced in, even where they border the roadside. The cultivation, too, is intensive to a degree really astonishing, not a square foot of soil being wasted. A French landscape in that district, viewed in the distance from rising ground, reminds one of nothing so much as a patchwork quilt made up of small irregular and varicoloured patches, relieved only by the big state high roads, all running very straight and invariably lined by the eternal and monotonously regular double rows of poplar and other trees.

In the smaller villages the streets are very rarely paved, in fact, the village usually consists of two rows of blank barn walls flanking the road on either side, with muddy little lanes running off at right angles to farms lying back from the road. The houses in these villages, or rather the farms, are all built in the form of a square, one side being formed by the one-storied dwelling house ; the others consisting of barns and stables, and the entire centre of the square is invariably occupied by a good old ripe dung-heap. You enter the yard through an archway between the two barns presenting blank walls to the roadway, and to get to the house, which is nearly always on the far side of the yard, you have to make your way carefully round three sides of the square along a three-foot wide cobbled ledge running round the manure heap. Woe betide the officer or man who came home late to his billet, and in the darkness forgot the odoriferous obstacle in the middle of the yard and made straight for the lights of the house, which he would see directly in front of him in passing through the archway.

Naours was just such a village, though it was a big and important one. It contained one or two quite superior houses belonging to the more prosperous farmers, but they were all of the same one-storied type built in the form of a square which I have endeavoured to describe, and though the central courtyard in some cases had been converted from its original purpose into a garden, in one instance with a really pretty little fountain in the middle, every one of them had the traditional manure heap somewhere on the premises. They were all farms of course, and I suppose that sort of thing is necessary in the intensive cultivation they practice in France, but it takes a lot of getting used to.

Wherever there are cross-roads in or near these villages you will find one or two little winehouses or estaminets, but there are no shops, as there are in even the smallest of hamlets at home. The French country folk, it would appear, go marketing once a month or thereabouts to the towns in their neighbourhood for the necessities they can't raise themselves, but mostly I think they are pretty well self-supporting. The same old church-going hat will serve madame for years, and she usually keeps it, as far as I noticed, in the original cardboard box under the bed in the '' best room,'' in the same place where she stores the family bread. On more than one occasion I have been awakened with apologies by madame about four o'clock in the morning, while she dug under the bed I was lying on for a hugh cartwheel loaf of bread.

I remember one Saturday afternoon all the local

notables of Naours turned out in full sporting rig ; green velveteen hunting suits, fat stockings or yellow leggings, Tyrolese hats with feathers stuck up behind, and all armed with guns.   The mayor was there, taking a leading part in the proceedings, and after a great deal of promenading and loitering around the village for the purpose of showing off their fine feathers, they all finally adjourned to the largest estaminet in the village, where they proceeded to spend a very jovial and convivial evening—in which we joined.   We couldn't understand at first what all this parade was about, but at length it turned out that this was merely a full-dress rehearsal for a hunt that was to take place the next day.   Early on the Sunday morning we were there to see them set out, which they did with great *eclat* and amidst much excitement on the part of the womenfolk, for the Foret de Naours, a large forest lying a few kilometers to the north of the village, where the hunt was to take place.   For all the preliminary parade and show, they evidently had some real good sport, for the party returned in the late evening with two boars they had bagged ; great ugly brutes with tusks—not unlike the bush pigs of which I afterwards saw many while on service in East Africa.

It seems that these boar hunts, at least in that part of Picardy, were regular communal affairs, specially organised for the purpose of keeping down the wild boars in the woods of the neighbourhood, which during the war had so increased in numbers in some districts as to become a nuisance to the farmers.   At night they would leave the shelter of the woods, and we were told they did a lot of damage to the fields in the vicinity of their haunts.   We often saw for ourselves their tracks in the fields bordering on woods and plantations, and many months after this hunt at Naours I saw a whole family of wild boars crossing a drive in the Bois de Auxi, near Auxi-le-Chateau.   The party consisted of Pa boar and Ma boar, with ten or twelve little striped boarlets sprinting along in the rear.

CHAPTER XXI

On the March—I am " Straffed "

In due course our three weeks rustication of Naours came to an end, and about the end of November 1916 the 15th Division started the return move towards the war. The 44th and 45th Brigades went into the front line first, and ours, the 46th, followed in reserve. The first move from Naours, as regards our own battalion, was to the town of Warloy, where we remained in billets for three or four days before going up into the immediate line reserve.

One little incident sticks in my memory in connection with the march from Naours to Warloy. Just as the battalion moved off from Naours, instructions arrived by mounted orderly from the brigadier for the adjutants of the different battalions of the brigade to meet him at the cross-roads near the village of Talmas. We rendez-voused there as instructed, were met by the brigadier and his staff, and in his company we rode forward to the part of the road he was going to select as the bivouacing ground for his brigade when it halted for the midday meal. His choice fell on a stretch of the road just before it entered the small town of Rubempre, and the exact bivouacing ground to be taken up by each battalion was personally allocated and pointed out to the adjutant concerned by the brigadier himself. On receipt of my own instructions I rode back to meet the battalion, and when we reached our appointed bivouacing area we formed column of companies, piled arms and bivouaced, with the battalion transport and company cookers all neatly parked in the rear. We were congratulating our-selves on having executed the manœuvre very smartly, but no sooner had we got settled down than up rode the brigadier (Brig.-Gen. Matheson) and let out on me with a deuce of a straffing for not carrying out his instructions to the letter. These instructions, it seemed, were that the first company of our battalion should be aligned with a certain telegraph post as numbered from a small farmhouse in the vicinity, and here were we bivouaced nearly two posts wide of the mark ! As a matter of fact, I had not heard the details of my instructions too clearly when the brigadier was allotting the ground, for the reason that the horse I was riding at the time had more oats than sense in him, and in his twistings and turnings about he wouldn't let me listen carefully to what the brigadier was saying. However, we unpiled arms, and at the '' short trail '' the complete battalion with transport, cookers, water-carts, etc., all in parked order moved forward a couple of hundred paces to our correct position.

General Matheson was a guardsman (Coldstreams), and I mention all this little incident in detail as showing again the result of the Guards training, which insists upon nicity of obedience in the smallest detail. And very rightly too, I thoroughly believe. An officer who is kept up to the scratch himself will likewise keep his men up to the scratch, and so discipline maintained rigidly from the top will knit the whole unit together, be it battalion, brigade or division.

CHAPTER XXII

Stagnant Trench Warfare and Misery

From Warloy, after three or four days in Divisional Reserve, we moved forward through the town of Albert to front line reserve, in which position we were accomodated in huts at Scott's Wood near the ruined village of Contalmaison. There we remained nearly a week before going into the trenches for what eventually turned out to be a ten weeks' spell of front line duty. For a week or two prior to the time I am now writing of, we had been having very cold wintry weather with a great deal of snow, but about this time a hard frost set in, which lasted without a break all the time we remained on the Somme front, that is, until about the end of February 1917. During these ten or twelve weeks the ground was frozen like iron ; so hard that trench digging was almost out of the question, and although very little fresh snow fell in that time the old snow lay dry and powdery. There was a biting east wind all the time, too. In fact, the weather was extremely severe, and ever since that winter spell in the open trenches I have a very keen sympathy for those poor Eskimo folks who live in the arctic regions. We used to think we should never again know what it was to be really warm and cosy ; that delightful feeling that seemed to us then to belong only to the remote pre-war days. Most of us, ours being a Scottish division, knew something of cold weather, but even in the worst of Scottish winters a man could always find shelter and warmth somewhere ; he had his home to go to at times, where he could at least depend on a warm meal and a comfortable bed at night, however it might blow and freeze out-of-doors. In those trenches we froze for days together, night and day alike. The only poor shelter

was in cowering down on the leeward side of the trenches,
("ditches" would be better description of them), so
as to escape the force of the biting wind that prevailed
from the east, and which, when one was exposed to the
full blast of it, laden as it was with the powdery dry snow,
felt as if it might cut one's ears off. These conditions
we had to endure day and night throughout a spell of duty
in the actual front line, sometimes for three or four days
on end. When we were in reserve or support the conditions were much better, the trenches farther back
being in fairly good repair and furnished with dugouts
and other accommodation in which the men were comparatively comfortable and able to obtain some sleep
when off duty. For the poor devils in those front-line
trenches, however, there was no real sleep ; just the sleep
of sheer exhaustion snatched while standing up on their
feet and leaning against a ground-sheet pegged to the
side of the ditch they were in.   They could not lie down,
because these ditches were more than ankle deep in frozen
slush, which was kept churned up all the time by the feet
of the men moving about.   The duck-boards we put down
were of little use ; they were soon trodden in and sub-
merged in the mud.   Although the surface of the ground
round about was frozen hard, it must be remembered
that we were in a valley, and the trenches there were not
dry like those farther back on the slope.

I should explain here that what we then held as our
front line, called in that part "Scotland Trench," just
in front of the village of Le Sars on the Albert-Bapaume
road, had been originally a hastily made trench captured
from the enemy. It had never been constructed with
proper revettments and dugouts, or anything to make it
a permanent line of defence ; it was in fact just a long
deep ditch. There were no communication trenches
to it from our side, or if there had been they had by this
time fallen in and were useless. After the heavy rains
in October and November those hurriedly constructed
trenches mostly collapsed, as it was found impossible
to keep them open and in a state of repair for their whole

length with the labour at our command. We therefore
maintained only short stretches of trench at intervals,
which were mis-called " strong-points " by the Brigade.
To us it seemed they were " damned weak points ! "
Each of those so-called " strong-points " was supposed
to be garrisoned by a platoon—but what puny little
remnants of platoons we put into them ! Some of our
platoons were so reduced by casualties and sickness
that they did not muster more than a dozen men, sometimes less. For a time our strength was so low that every
available " employed " man was mustered for his turn
of duty in the front line, including even the commanding
officer's batman.

To say that the men were miserable at the time I
am now writing about is to put it mildly. To anyone
who did not actually experience it, the shocking conditions and the misery our men were enduring in some
parts of the front line trenches throughout that hard
winter on the Somme must be well-nigh inconceivable.
I have on more than one occasion found men weeping
from sheer misery, and who could blame them ? Among
them were men well over army age, and men who had
never been accustomed to roughing it. As I said before,
it is one thing to experience a hard winter at home, where
one can always get in somewhere out of the cold, and
where a man usually can get a hot meal. It is quite
another thing to be out exposed to the cold for days at a
stretch, without any shelter to speak of, and without hot
food. Worst of all, with little or no sleep. The want of
sleep tells on even the strongest man before long and
reduces him to a pretty weak creature ; the continued
lack of sleep soon takes the starch out of him and saps
the morale.

As an officer and company commander, I did not, of
course, spend the whole of my time in the front line points
I am endeavouring to describe. I was able to get back
at intervals to an ex-German dugout some two or three
hundred yards behind the actual front line, where our
company headquarters were established. I did not go

there for the purpose of taking refuge from the enemy and the weather, but because it was company headquarters, and a company commander had a great deal of executive duties to carry out even when in the front line. Throughout the twenty-four hours there were various reports that had to be sent in at fixed intervals to battalion headquarters, with whom we were connected by field telephone. Yet for all that I and the other officers were able to get into a dugout for short spells now and then, I sometimes used to think that I would give years of my life for one long really satisfying sleep in a warm bed between clean sheets. If I felt like that, who can describe the feelings of the poor " other ranks " sticking it out in the frozen open all the time ? True, when they came back to support or reserve they had no responsibilities, whereas an officer's duties never ended. Many of our privates were men of education who might have made good officers, but I think some of them were averse to taking a commission simply because they shirked the continual responsibilities. Casualties among officers, also, were higher in proportion than those sustained by the rank and file.

I mentioned that I would have given years of my life for a good sleep. But what did years of our lives mean to us then ? The good old pre-war days seemed very far away ; done and finished with like the closed pages of a book. Those of us who kept on surviving death and wounds and sickness felt that, according to all the laws of chance, our turn must come sooner or later, in what form we did not know nor care. We had become more or less fatalists, and we had got to look upon the war as the normal state of our existence. Death and wounds had become a joke with us. We could not then conceive that some day the war might end and the world return to something like the old state of things, leaving us free to do as we liked with our lives and bodies. The best we could hope for was a " blighty " wound that would take us out of it for a spell. When I say that self-inflicted " blighties " were not unknown, it will give an idea of the lengths some of the weaker-kneed were prepared to go in an attempt to get out of the trenches and away from it all. When a man deliberately blows part of his own hand or foot off, he surely must be in a very miserable and depressed state of mind. Men proved to have inflicted wounds upon themselves were very severely dealt with. A more common and far simpler plan of the " trench-dodgers " at that time was to endeavour deliberately to contract trench-foot. In our part of the line that was easy, in fact, it was difficult to avoid, but in other and drier sectors also the practice was fairly rife. So much so that a divisional order was at one time issued to the effect that a platoon officer would forfeit his leave should any of his men be invalided with trench-foot. That of course, was grossly unfair.

CHAPTER XXIII

HOLDING A WEAK LINE WITH WINTER'S HELP

DURING all this time, although the communications to the front line were so bad, our rations came up every night regularly, and they were ample. We also got our daily rum ration, which was served out in tots under the personal supervision of the company commander at the " stand-to " before dawn. At least, that was the procedure in my own company. I thoroughly believe that that rum ration in the early morning, after a frozen night, saved many a life. Very few men refused it, although sometimes I was told by some of them, especially the young fellows, that they had been teetotal before they joined the army, and would be again if they survived. In that attitude they were of course right, and I admired them for it. I certainly think that, principles or no, these men had sound sense, and that the small daily dose of alcohol in those conditions had the effect intended by H.M. Government's medical advisers. There were a few staunch teetotalers, the rabid kind, not many, however, who stuck out for their principles and refused to take the rum ration. It was very touching to observe how kind some of our old soldiers were to those die-hards !

Although our rations were ample, the men had to eat them cold ; they had no means as a rule in the front line of warming up their food. This lack of an occasional hot meal told on them, and it is the main reason so many contracted trench-foot and other ailments due to bad circulation. Having pushed forward our line so far into the old German ground in the big attacks during the previous months, our communications were very bad, and it was almost an impossible undertaking to get up hot food to the men in the front line. Divisional headquarters did what they could, and there were things called "hot-food containers," big hermetically closed tanks strapped to a man's back, which were used in an attempt to get hot tea or soup up to the front. The fortunate men who were first served out of these containers got their tea or soup hot enough, but once the container was opened the contents soon became cold ; long before all the men had been served.

I have gone to some lengths in attempting to give a picture of the conditions we experienced during that terrible winter on our part of the Somme front, and I do not think I have exaggerated. It was sheer misery personified. Yet the moral of our men remained wonderfully good, all things considered. Despite what they had to suffer they stuck it well, mostly without a word of complaint. There was the usual small percentage of grousers, of course (some soldiers would grouse if they found themselves in heaven), but there were others who would have dropped on their feet without a word, and some did. The country should thank God that the latter were in the majority.

I never once heard of any of our men deserting to the enemy. On the other hand, it was no uncommon thing at the time I am writing of for Germans to come over and give themselves up, usually singly, but sometimes in parties of two or three, or even more. These enemy desertions usually occurred after dark, naturally, and from the fact that the Germans almost invariably carried their packs it would seem they seized the opportunity of deserting while a relief was in progress. Once in Scotland trench a German came over to us in broad daylight. He was only a young boy, and he came running down the side of the Bapaume road across the stretch of three or four hundred yards that separated our lines at that point ; stumbling and crouching and trying to take cover in the ditch along the side of the road, but in a panic of fright and sobbing like a baby all the while. Their snipers did their damndest to get him, but the kid managed to win through to us. He was a good-looking boy, and he spoke English well. Some of our Jocks wanted to keep him as a mascot, but that of course couldn't be allowed, and he was sent back along with other prisoners. He was hungry, as in fact were all the Germans who came over to us.

On another occasion we found four Germans living in a dugout in Le Sars village among the ruins not far behind us. They said they had been there for three or four days, and they eventually came out and gave themselves up because they were starving. Once two Russians came over. They were part of a batch of prisoners from the eastern front, who were working on the roads behind the German lines in front of us. Lousy specimens they were too.

As I mentioned before, our front line at that time was merely a detached string of " strong-points," and these Germans must have come across between these points without being seen by our men. They were lucky ! It could easily be done, however ; I myself, in going over to our front line on a very dark night, have wandered on until stopped by the crack of a badly aimed German rifle almost in my face. Our front was supposed to be protected by a strong continuous belt of barbed-wire, but the wire in parts took some finding, as can readily be imagined when people could walk right across without noticing any to speak of. There was of course a lot of loose derelict wire lying all over " no-man's-land," where it had been blown about by shell fire, but that could easily be got through, and it could by no means be looked upon as a belt of protective wire. At that time on the Somme the front trench H.Q. of every company in our division was provided with a big-ledger-like book called a " trench report " book—the idea of some methodical " clerk general " on the staff, I suppose. These books were indexed like an accounts ledger, and under " W " (Wiring) every company commander in our sector for weeks past seemed to have recorded hundreds of yards of wiring done by his company each night. If that book was to be believed, we should have had a thick impenetratable belt of wire sufficient to keep back the whole German army. Yet we could wander in the dark bang slap up to the German trenches without encountering any wire of ours worth noticing ! Speaking of the same comic "trench report books," in one of them I once noticed under the index letter " R " (Reliefs) an entry —" I wonder if the Germans are as relieved when they are relieved as we are ! "

I have said something about our front line string of disconnected strong-points, which we, who had to garrison and hold them, called " bloody weak points ! " Our main reason for that, and it was a good one, was that there being no communication trenches leading to these points, we could only reach them by going across the open after dark. We sometimes did so singly or in very small parties during the day, by sprinting and dodging from shell hole to shell hole, but that was hazardous and only done in cases of necessity, The German snipers, with their telescopic rifle sights, were pretty deadly unless one knew how to dodge by darting in sprints diagonally from hole to hole, so as to give them no time to get " a bead on." Even then a lot of our men lost their lives in trying to get across during the daylight. These so-called strong points were death traps, for the reason that while the snow lay on the ground, as it did for weeks on end, the enemy airmen easily spotted the tracks leading to them and they marked them down accordingly for the information of their artillery. As a result, the German gunners, would at times fill in a slack morning by concentrating on these points one by one and deliberately trying to pound them out of existence. I have seen their shells from more than one battery concentrated for an hour on end on one of these isolated posts of ours, and yet we could do nothing for the poor devils in it beyond telephoning the brigade to get our own artillery on to the opposing batteries. While those bombardments were in progress our men couldn't leave their posts, neither could we reach them ;

they just had to sit tight and take it. When at long last the dusk fell and we were able to get over with the stretcher bearers, God knows we too often came upon a dreadful sight. The dead were beyond it all ; we could only extricate them from the blown-in trench and bury them, equipment and all as they lay, in a near-by shell hole. But men wounded in the early part of the day perhaps had to wait there until dark before we could get them out and sent back to a dressing station. Often they just died, when a little timely help might have saved them. I saw a man who in the morning had had his arm nearly blown off near the elbow, and yet he was waiting patiently there in that mud hole throughout the remainder of the bombardment until he could be taken out hours later. Fortunately for him, some of his comrades in that same '' strong-point '' knew something about first aid and ligatures. I never heard whether he survived, but of course he was only one of many.

CHAPTER XXIV

MOSTLY GROUSES

WAR is not and never has been a kid glove affair, but we used to wonder sometimes whether it is not being carried too far nowadays. In the old days the fighting men were mostly professional soldiers, and they fought openly and above board by appointment beforehand. Every warrior within a radius of a hundred miles or more had early notice of when a battle was to be fought, and it was his own fault if he wasn't there to time. But they never deliberately slaughtered one another in batches in cold blood in the way we do nowadays ; at least, not unless they had a real good reason for it. I mean, they didn't slaughter poor devils who couldn't lift a finger to help themselves, and who had done nothing more to deserve it than that their country was at war, for reasons mostly beyond their comprehension. The old-time soldiers, from what I have read, were too sporting for that sort of thing.

I am not blaming the German artillery for what they did. I've no doubt our own artillery did the same to them when they could, and were glad of the chance. I'm merely wondering what the old-time soldiers would say about modern warfare if they could see it. It seems to me there is something wrong with a civilisation in which —during peace time—people get all greatly excited and waste reams of newspaper space over a petty-fogging little murder committed naturally in a moment of passion —in which mass meetings with prayers are held outside a gaol on the hanging of a murderer who probably thoroughly deserves it ; and yet, let some men called politicians sign a paper called a " declaration of war," and those same hysterical people instantly become equally hysterical

G

in applauding the wholesale execution by hundreds and thousands of their fellow men, mostly men just like themselves, who never thought of committing murder until it became legalised and in fact compulsory. At the word " war " it appears that civilised man is ready and eager to relapse back into the old savagery, but without any of the chivalry shown by the old-time professional roughnecks—the so-called barbarians. I'm talking of course of the people at home ; not of the troops, of the people who were responsible for the war primarily, but who did not themselves have to get down into the muck of it. When I got my first leave some months after the time I am now writing about, I noticed that the most bloodthirsty war critics at home were those men who knew, or felt fairly confident, that they could not be called up for service. Their rage against the Germans in some cases was terrible to behold !

We troops when we were back from the line often used to discuss this sort of thing. The general conclusion was that the old methods of warfare were better and cleaner. As for instance, when King Robert of Scotland before the battle of Bannockburn fought a single-handed duel to the death with the chosen English champion, de Bohoun, in full view of both armies. That must have been worth seeing, we thought. We would have liked to see a similar show put up by batches of staff officers, those superior beings who sat in comfort in chateaux far behind the line, and who, apparently spent all their time in devising operations such as the big attacks on the Somme with their appalling loss of life, down to the little battalion and company raids in which the results gained very seldom justified the losses sustained in carrying them out. However, I suppose that was their job, and lives were cheap.

By way of digression while on this subject ; those idle confabs of the men on the good old by-gone days of straightforwarɔ fighting sometimes led to quaint discussions. One Jock was puzzled to know how the old-time soldier in full armour managed to scratch himself when he was lousy! Perhaps he was unaware that war at one time may have been a more gentlemanly and cleanly affair than in these modern days of high civilisation.

Speaking of the artillery, I have always had the greatest admiration for that branch of the service, but sometimes we didn't like their methods. We particulary hated their so-called "artillery duels." The announcement in the Corps Intelligence (" Comic Cuts "), or in the home papers, that our artillery in a certain sector had carried out a duel with the enemy artillery might have sounded very businesslike, but we poor infantry only too often knew what it meant. An artillery duel seemed to us to be a sort of mutual arrangement between both sides that " we'll pound your P.B.I. and you can pound ours." If by any chance one side, that is the artillery, (the P.B.I. had no say in the matter!) were unsporting enough to start on a bit of counter-battery work directly against the opposing artillery, the artillery men on the other side would leave their guns and retire to their deep dugouts and refuse to play!

I daresay I'm being sarcastic now, and perhaps rather unfair on the staff and artillery, but that is how it seemed to us infantrymen then. There is no doubt that the infantry bore the brunt of it all, and although a due meed of credit must be given to the other branches of the services, the infantry were the " cannon-fodder," and it was on the infantry that everything depended. The other branches, although indispenable, were after all auxiliary to the infantry. Infantry can carry on a war against infantry, as has often happened, but the other branches of an army such as artillery, engineers, and even the new tanks, cannot fight one another to a conclusion without the help of the P.B.I. in clearing up for them.

As a matter of fact, our artillery were really good, and we were only too often glad of their support. What they accomplished was marvellous when it is remembered that by far the great majority of their officers had only learnt that highly technical branch of warfare since the outbreak.

Their barrage work latterly was as a rule wonderfully accurate, as those infantrymen knew who had to advance within fifty or a hundred yards of the line of bursting shells, and at the same rate of advance too. Of course some guns were worn out and inaccurate, and some artillery officers were not too good at mathematics, with the result that our own infantry at times got what was intended for the Boches. As often as not it was our own fault, however, ; I mean the fault of the leading wave of infantry, in advancing at a faster rate than that laid down for the barrage, and so coming under our own shell fire. It was sometimes very difficult to judge with any degree of accuracy the correct rate of advance on these occasions, but we and the artillery both benefited in time from the experience gained in the early Somme offensives.

All the time, we didn't like those artillery " duels "— they were distinctly nasty from our point of view. But then, we were only the P.B.I.

CHAPTER XXV

THE EERIE AQUEDUCT ROAD

ABOUT a couple of hundred yards or so behind our front line there was a sunken road leading out from the ruined village of Le Sars. It was there that the two old German dugouts occupied by our company headquarters and signallers were situated, but at that part the road cutting widened out into a sort of shallow valley about sixty to a hundred yards wide, with fairly steep banks on either side. The dugouts were both on the same side, and having originally been constructed by the enemy, the entrances to them now faced the wrong way for us, being fully exposed to the enemy artillery and machine gun fire. The whole of that area and the exact position of every dugout in it was, of course, well known to the Germans, it having so recently been within their own front, and they made full use of that knowledge. They were continually putting over stuff into this little valley, and sometimes without any warning a whole salvo of shells would skim the bank and land plunk in the middle of the road. God help any troops that happened to be there just then. This systematic salvo firing usually took place at night, when the Germans well knew that the movement of reliefs would be in progress under cover of the dark. Too often they caught parties of our men moving across to the shelter of the opposite bank. The dugouts occupied by us were marked down for special attention. A " whizz-bang " would often land right at the entrance, but worst of all were the fixed rifles they had trained on these entrances. As our line bent backwards on our left and the Boches were occupying the higher ground, from one part of their trenches (called the Gallwitz Line) they could overlook and enfilade the

whole of our part of the sunken road. It was there
that they had those fixed rifles, that is, rifles that had
been carefully sighted during the day-time on the dugout
entrances and then firmly clamped into that position,
so that at any time of the night a sentry had only to pull
the trigger and the bullet hit the mark. At intervals
during the night when we were in the dugout we would
hear the smack of a bullet against the woodwork frame
of the entrance. We were continually moving in and out
of the dugout throughout the night, and it certainly gave
a most exhilarating " goosey " feeling down the spine as
you squeezed yourself through the broken-down entrance,
wondering whether the German sentry was going to take
it into his head to let off one just then. Several officers
and orderlies were killed by those chance shots in the
night.

One night a small party of Royal Engineers consisting
of an officer, a sergeant and two men, accompanied by
an officer of the Scottish Rifles, came up to our front on
some special duty. I can't say now what that duty was,
but I think it was intended to construct some dugouts
in the other bank, that is, on the sheltered side of the
sunken road. However, they never got started, because
they were just in time to meet one of the Boche " whizz-
bang" salvoes. I was over at our front line—the "strong-
points "—when it happened, but I came back about five
minutes later while they were trying to clear up the mess.
Of the Scottish Rifle officer no trace could be found in the
dark. Shortly afterwards, as I was getting down on
my hands and knees to lower myself backwards into the
dugout entrance, I found him—at least, part of him.

That sunken road was an eerie place and a decidedly
unhealthy neighbourhood. It was at its eeriest in the
dark hours before the dawn ; when everything seemed
so still and quiet, and pitch dark in the hollow except
for the faint gleam of the snow, palely illuminated every
now and then on the crests of the banks by the reflection
of an enemy verey light. One never knew when a shell
would come over with a " whoof " like the breath of

death—or whether one's guts would be stirred up by a bullet while clambering in or out of that awful dugout.

The whole of that wintry ten weeks or so spell of front line duty was not spent by us in Scotland trench and its nasty neighbourhood, which formed part of the left half of the front held by the 15th Division. Once or twice we were moved from the support trenches to the other half of the divisional front lying to the right of Le Sars village, that is, to the right of the Albert-Bapaume road, which ran through Le Sars. The trenches and support area on that side weren't quite so bad, comparatively speaking, except on the extreme right where they followed the track down into the hollow leading to the hamlet of Eaucourt l'Abbey. The 9th Division were in touch with us on that side.

In front of Le Sars South trench, immediately to the right of the Bapaume road, there was a piece of high ground called the Butte de Warlencourt, which was held in strength by the enemy. It was honeycombed by their observation posts and machine gun emplacements, from which they could overlook our trenches in the lower lying ground. That Butte was a queer sort of hill; as symmetrical in shape as a pyramid, and one would have thought it was an old slag-heap, except that there were no traces of any mining ever having been carried on in that neighbourhood. I came to the conclusion that it must be a big prehistoric tumulus. Anyhow, their observation posts and machine gunners on it gave us a lot of trouble, and for that reason it was often subjected to heavy shelling and was occasionally raided by our troops. In the course of these operations it was captured once or twice and cleared of its garrison, but the hill was never retained permanently by us because it was too far within the enemy lines, and as all the openings to the dugouts and tunnels were on their side, and of course fully exposed to their fire if held by us, it was untenable. Therefore we could only shell and raid the Butte now and then so as to discourage them from making too much

use of it. I remember one such night raid was carried
out on rather a big scale by our 45th Brigade. The
ground being still covered with snow, the troops taking
part in the raid were provided with '' camouflage ''
gowns like long white nightshirts. They also white-
washed their steel helmets. There was great merriment
when just before going over they mustered in the front
trenches like a big parade of ghosts. The raid was a
success, but the casualties on both sides were heavy.
Before that night was over, real ghosts were floating up
like the bubbles in sodawater.

I ought to mention that at this time on that part of
the Somme the big offensives had ceased, and we were
merely holding the line—with only nightly patrols and
occasional raids, and such like small shows to keep up our
circulation and prevent us from freezing. It was what
the newspapers and armchair critics at home called a
'' period of stagnation ! ''

About Christmas time 1916 I was again acting as
adjutant of the battalion, and although all home leave
for the infantry on our part of the Somme front was
stopped indefinitely, I obtained four days leave to
Paris. Two other officers got leave at the same time,
and needless to say we made the most of it. We had
saved up and borrowed until we accumulated what we
thought was an awful lot of francs, but as things turned
out it wasn't nearly enough, and I had to wire home
for more. On the expiration of the four days I was glad
to creep back to the Somme for peace and quiet and to
recuperate !

CHAPTER XXVI

We Move to the Arras Front

ABOUT the end of January 1917 the 15th Division, together with the 9th and several other divisions, was withdrawn from the Somme for good and transferred to the Arras front, where business was to be brightened up as we soon learnt. We did not know that at the time, of course, but we certainly were glad at getting out of those awful Somme trenches at last, even although we thought then it was only for a spell in reserve. The weather was still very cold and the snow lay on the ground almost continuously, but it was dry and clear, and decidedly bracing—when one could get out of it and into a decent billet now and then!

We moved back by stages through Albert and Millencourt to billets in a village lying to the north of Warloy. There I went sick with ague; a return of the old African fever I suppose. I had suffered from occasional attacks of ague for some weeks previously, but this time, now that we were completely out of the front line, they packed me off to hospital in Rouen. Shall I ever forget the hot bath I had on arrival at the hospital—in a real bathroom with everything complete; not out of a bucket or in a shell hole full of dirty cold water—and the blissful luxury of getting between clean linen sheets in a real bed! With all that pampering I was quite well again within two or three days, but they kept me there as a convalescent for about a week altogether. That time I spent in pottering around Rouen with an Australian Officer with whom I became chummy.

The first day we were allowed out we went to see Rouen Cathedral, about which I had read a lot. We had no difficulty at all in finding it, and after walking round for a while admiring the beautiful old building we moved on to look for a cafe. We hadn't gone far till, on turning a corner into an open square, we came upon another cathedral, even finer than the first, so we had to start our admiration all over again! Neither of them was *The* Cathedral. The fact is that Rouen has many fine old churches besides the famous cathedral, any one of which might pass for a cathedral in another town. The real cathedral, when we found it, although extremely interesting, I thought rather disappointing for the reason that it is so hemmed in by other buildings clustering close up against it that the whole effect of the beautiful ancient architecture is lost. There is no point from which one can view the building as a whole.

From the hospital I was transferred to the depot camp at Rouen, and after two days there another officer and myself were detailed to conduct a large party of assorted troops to the 4th Army Echelon Base at Etaples. We had rather a job with these troops, the majority of whom were Australians; an undisciplined lot. As we were entraining them at Rouen station into the usual goods wagons used for the transport of troops (marked on the outside " 8 Chevaux—40 Hommes ! ") the whole lot of them started baa-ing like sheep as they flocked up the gangways into the wagons! However, we arrived at Etaples the next day all present and correct, and handed over our flock to the Camp Adjutant.

The next day, together with my batman Porter, who had been with me all the time, I was sent on to rejoin the 15th Division, which I was informed had by then moved up to reserve behind the Arras front. We travelled by train to St. Pol, and on arrival there I learnt from the Railway Transport Officer that the 15th Division was in billets in the neighbourhood of Aubigny, about half way between St. Pol and Arras. He was only about twenty kilometers out in his information, as I found to my discomfort within the next twelve or thirteen hours. However, Porter and I started off, and just after leaving St. Pol we got a lift on a G.S. wagon as far as Tinques, from

where we struck north on foot to Aubigny. On arrival
at that place no one seemed to know anything of the
whereabouts of the 15th Division, although there were
a lot of other Scottish troops in the neighbourhood, so
we had to beat it back to Tinques and the main road,
where I found an A.S.C. officer who told me that my own
battalion was at a village some kilometers to the south.
He too was wrong! To cut it short, we spent the whole
evening and night in trudging along searching for the 15th
Division and our own unit, the 12th Highland Light
Infantry, and it was not until near dawn that we
eventually tracked them down in a little obscure place
called Izel-lez-Hamel, a village I had never heard of
before. We found it more by sheer luck than good
guidance. We were so utterly dog-tired when we arrived
that I threw myself down just as I was on the bare brick
floor of the farm kitchen in which our company officers
were billetted, and fell sound asleep instantly. I am
mentioning all this to show the lack of efficiency on
the part of some transport officers and others in such-like
cushey jobs, whose business it was to know the movement
and location of units in their area.

Had we been on a main road all the time in our pere-
grinations that night, we might have got a lift in some
army car or wagon, but in all that long tramping about,
since we left the wagon at Tinques in the early afternoon, the only assistance we got was a short ride on top
of a big howitzer gun. The gun, which was hitched to a
traction engine, was a huge affair with caterpillar wheels,
and when we first came upon it it had stopped at a cross-
roads. As it appeared to be going in the same direction
as ourselves we thankfully clambered up on top, but we
very soon wished we were off it ! Anyone who has had
a ride perched on top of a giant howitzer clanking and
bumping over a bad road will know it is not the ideal
vehicle for comfortable travelling. Once it had started
we could not get off ; it took us all our time to cling like
grim death to the great juggernaut, our teeth rattling
all the while so that we couldn't even speak ! For-

tunately, it stopped again after a kilometer or so, and we ruefully lowered ourselves to the ground and resumed our journey on foot, feeling very stiff and sore.

The battalion remained about a week at Izel-lez-Hamel after I rejoined, and we had quite a pleasant time in that pretty little out-of-the-way French village, the weather having turned mild and Springlike. The men were kept hard at work with drills and exercises, of course, but they were in comparatively comfortable billets, and they had the whole of the afternoons for football and other sports, in which they were encouraged. About this time we received several new drafts of officers and men, and we gradually assumed the strength of a full battalion once again. In these drafts were included many of our own men who had been invalided with wounds or sickness during the preceding months on the Somme, and we were glad to have them back, but the majority of the men composing the drafts that came to us about that time and for a while after were men of the original old regular 1st and 2nd Battalions of the Highland Light Infantry. When the Arras offensive was in full swing I believe our battalion, the 12th H.L.I., included far more of the old regular soldiers than did either the 1st or 2nd Battalions at that time. A hard lot they were too, but fine soldiers.

CHAPTER XXVII

"Bantams"

While on the subject of drafts, I think I have omitted to mention the draft of "bantams" that joined us the previous August or September while we were in the Somme sector. In the early stages of the war two "Bantam" battalions of the Highland Light Infantry were raised at Glasgow. It was considered, I suppose, that a small man could handle a rifle against the enemy quite as effectively as a bigger man, which seems sound enough in theory, but in actual practice there is a great deal more to be done in warfare than merely shooting down the enemy. That is the culmination to which the whole of an army's tremendous activities are directed, of course, but unfortunately the actual shooting point is only occasionally reached—otherwise wars would cost less. Anyhow, the two bantam battalions were broken up eventually and their details drafted to the various service battalions. Our share of the little men was a fairly big one, and I remember the majority of them bore names beginning with "Mac." Not that they were more Scotch than the rest of our men, but it seemed we had been allocated the "Mac" section of the roll at the base depot !

These bantams were not welcomed by us. They gave us a great deal of trouble and made things difficult for us in many ways. Not that the little fellows themselves were always to blame, because it surely is not to be expected that an undersized man can carry the full field equipment and do the strenuous work that nowadays is enough to tax the strength even of a full-grown soldier. The fact remains, however, that the small men were continually falling out on the march, or else the trench

fire-steps were too low for them ; and generally speaking
they often proved more of a hindrance than anything
else. Worst of all was when they got stuck in the deep
sticky mud of the communication trenches during night
reliefs, as quite often happened. Nothing was more
exasperating than for the relief column to be held up on
these occasions, especially on a dirty wet night when the
enemy artillery was active. During these delays, when
the word was passed back " Bantam stuck in the mud,"
a growl would sometimes be heard from the blackness
in the rear " Tramp the little b.... in ! " At that time
whale-oil was issued to the troops daily for the purpose
of greasing their feet and legs to prevent " trench-foot."
For a while we thought we would require to make an
extra issue of whale-oil to the bantams to prevent
" trench-bottom ! "

Perhaps I am being too hard on our bantams. If so,
it is because of the unfortunate fact that there were so
many downright little " stiffs " in the batch that joined
us—real hard cases—street corner boys from the slums of
Glasgow. For all that, I must say the majority were
excellent soldiers when at last we did manage to get them
up against the enemy and give them a chance of doing
a bit of actual fighting. They were keen-witted mostly,
and they were far more adept at foraging and looking
after themselves under difficult conditions than were the
regulation sized soldiers. Some of these bantams, as I
have said, were real bad cases—the under-nourished
and degenerate material that supplies the slum
" gangsters " of our cities. These worthies, whenever
we succeeded in getting them over the top, always
seemed rather charmed with the idea of being provided
with the opportunity of doing a little legalised murder,
without the fear of any interference on the part of their
natural enemies the police ! On the other hand, a considerable proportion of the bantams were small men
who had joined up voluntarily and who really were eager
to do their best, although, unfortunately for us and them,
the exertions demanded of the modern soldier proved to

be beyond their physical strength. There was also a sprinkling of young boys who obviously had falsified their ages when enlisting in the army, and some of these youths were little heroes. Early in 1917 an army order was issued to return under-age soldiers to their parents, if claimed by the latter, or to a special training depot that had been formed at the Etaples base to receive them (what we called the " Boys' Brigade ! ") but a few of these boys stoutly held to the lie about their age and refused point-blank to leave the battalion and the front line ! They were the real stuff, and we did our best to take care of them.

We tried to make things easy for all our bantams, but a lot took advantage of that special consideration, and they seemed to think the plea " A'm a bantam, sir " covered all sorts of delinquencies. I remember one of these bad bargains, on his n'teenth appearance before the commanding officer, when asked whether he had anything to say, started out on a long rigmarole " Yes, sir, A'm a bantam, sir, I dinna ken whit they N.C.O.'s is comin' to nowadays, sir, this is a con-spire-acy, sir, etc., etc ! "

It took us a long time to use up that draft of bantams, and a few of the hard cases stuck to us throughout—it seemed that nothing less than a pole-axe could ever lay them out. But despite all our grousings about them when we were on the march, or when they were mis-behaving in billets, we were often glad to have the little chaps at a pinch.

CHAPTER XXVIII

ARRAS—A CITY UNDER SHELL-FIRE

SOME time about the middle of February we moved up to Arras for our first spell of front line duty in that sector. It was late in the afternoon as we marched through the town of Duisans, and not long after passing that place we noticed from the increasing clamour of the guns, and the reflection of enemy verey lights in the gathering dusk away to our half-left, that we were once again approaching the war. The road we were on, one of the big arterial roads of France, was full of traffic ; endless lines of infantry, artillery, and every branch of the army were moving in a continuous stream in both directions, and we were quite surprised to see a number of French civilian market wagons in the procession. For some kilometers before reaching the town of Arras, the northern side of the road, that is, the side exposed to the enemy, was screened all the way by big camouflage nets stretched along the roadside. It was quite dark by the time we entered the city of Arras through the old Western Porte ; a kind of Roman triumphal arch, though I don't know what it was built to commemorate.

As we proceeded farther into the city we were halted in one of the main streets to await the guides detailed to conduct the battalion to our billets, and I remember that while we waited there, still in column of route but standing easy, with plenty of time to look around us, we were astonished at the busy night life of the place. Everything was in pitch darkness, of course, but the streets were full of troops and we could see that a number of shops were open for business, although windows and doors were carefully screened so as not to throw any light out on the street. Having just come from the Somme, where the front line was removed from the nearest civilian life by desolate miles, it amazed us to see all this bustle and signs of civilian activity so close to the fighting line. It must be remembered that at that time the German trenches were hard up against the city of Arras ; in fact, to the left of our front and down towards the River Scarpe the front line trenches actually cut through the outlying suburbs ; right through the ruins of houses and factories, and all that remained of that devastated part of the town. However, more on that subject later.

Our battalion was billetted in the neighbourhood of the Theatre Place, and my own company headquarters was in a house almost opposite the house in which Robespierre, the " Attorney of Arras," was born. Like most of the other houses in that area it had been knocked about a lot by the Boche guns, but I remember noticing the memorial brass plate on the wall. Because of its historical associations, we thought of shifting our quarters over to the old house, but after an inspection of it we decided to stay where we were, although both houses appeared to belong to the same period. These ancient houses as a rule are uncomfortable billets, especially when they are swarming with rats. At the time I couldn't help wondering what the ghost of Robespierre would have thought of British soldiers rummaging and poking about his old home and the other old houses in the neighbourhood that must have been so familiar to him. Robespierre had no great love for the British in his lifetime. What tales might have been told by the old rooms of that house of the secret meetings and conspiracies once held within their walls ; secret doings that altered the whole course of the world's history and convulsed Europe for twenty years ?

It took us a long time to get over our first astonishment at the civilian life that still existed in Arras early in 1917 despite the close proximity of the front line and the frequent bombardment of the city by the Germans. And yet the German trenches had been right up against

the outskirts of Arras for over two years. The marvel
is that so much of the city remained standing at the time
I am writing of. Some parts of the town were in utter
ruins, of course, especially towards the suburb of Blangy
on the River Scarpe, and on the northern and eastern
sides. Throughout the city the majority of the buildings had been more or less badly knocked about by shellfire, but there were still many fine houses, and in fact
whole streets, that showed little if any sign of damage.
Why these neighbourhoods should have escaped the
repeated bombardments is a puzzle. Perhaps they were
sheltered in some way from the general direction of the
enemy artillery fire, although I never could see how that
came about. The city of Arras is fairly flat, and all
parts of it seemed to us equally exposed to the bombardments that came from the rising ground to the east,
or from the Vimey ridge immediately north of the River
Scarpe.

However, that may be, it was certainly evident that
in a bombardment it is the upper stories of the taller
houses that suffer most. The trajectory of falling
howitzer shells may be fairly steep, but in a crowded
town there is usually the top part of some building to
intercept them. The result is that the higher buildings
are whittled down from the top chunk by chunk, while
their lower stories and the smaller houses in between are
comparatively safe, though anyone with sense will keep
out of the streets while shells are coming over. More
people are hurt by falling masonry than by the actual
shell splinters. It is for that reason that a few bombs
dropped from aeroplanes may cause much more loss of
life than a heavy artillery bombardment.

As a matter of fact, I don't think the war could have
been carried on very " intensively " during the long
period the French troops held that part of the line. We
were often told that there had been a much larger civilian
population remaining in Arras right up to the time the
British took over that area. However, it seemed to us
at first a very " cushey " kind of warfare compared to

what we had experienced throughout the previous winter on the Somme, and what particularly charmed us was the comparative absence of mud and the ease with which the firing line could be reached. We had only to walk along the pavements and step into the trenches around the corner, as it were, instead of the wearisome treks in the dark across miles of mud and desolation that a trench relief entailed on the Somme.

Mud we had become thoroughly accustomed to on the Somme. It had seemed to us the normal condition to be literally plastered with thick clayey mud from head to foot for days on end. What a change this was especially for the men belonging to the kilted battalions ; men who knew what it was to have the hairs torn by the roots from their nether limbs by dried mud when they moved after a short spell of rest. Often I have seen kilted soldiers carefully crumbling away the caked mud from their knees before rising from their seats in a dugout. When I say that the Arras trenches were free from mud I am speaking in a comparative sense ; there was mud in plenty there too in wet weather, but instead of being thickly and continually encased in if we were merely well smeared, and there were plenty of opportunities for cleaning ourselves.

We certainly thought the Arras front a great improvement on the conditions we had up till then become used to, but although we didn't know it at first, we had been moved to that sector for a special purpose, and in the course of a few short weeks there were abundant signs that a " liveliness " might be expected. If we had any illusions when we first arrived at Arras that it was to continue for us a quiet and rather interesting backwater of the war, they were soon rudely dispelled.

CHAPTER XXIX

WAR-BLASE FRENCH CIVILIANS

THIS narrative seems to be a series of digressions, and not being of a literary turn I find it difficult to keep to the main thread. But maybe these sidelights on the war, as seen from the point of view of an amateur soldier, may be as worthy of mention as accounts of the actual fighting. Anyhow, I think I should say something more about the conditions obtaining in the city of Arras as it was before the big April offensive started in earnest. We had seen many villages and hamlets utterly blotted out on the Somme (we ourselves had a lot to do with the blotting out of some of them !) and we knew what the town of Albert suffered, but these were small places compared with a large and important city such as Arras. Moreover, we never had the same opportunity of observing the conditions in them as we had at Arras, where even when in brigade support to the actual firing line we were living right in the heart of the city, instead of in old dilapidated German trenches or in roughly constructed shelters out in the open waste.

There must have been a considerable number of French civilians still in Arras at the time I am writing of, but I don't remember ever seeing any official figures, and as they mostly kept to their underground cellars, or at least out of sight during the daytime, it was hard to form even a rough estimate of the number of those patriots who chose to stick to their homes in the face of the enemy. A lot of them I daresay were spies, and every now and then we heard of these gentry being gathered in by our military police, but the great majority I think stuck on and braved the shells and hardships merely because of the huge profits they were making out of the troops.

There were many others, however, who remained for purely sentimental reasons; old folks who could or would not tear themselves away from their old homes; always holding out and living in cellars in a state of semi-starvation in the hope that eventually there might be no necessity for them to move. Food for these people in the ordinary way was scarce and very dear, and they could not have existed but for the surplus rations they got from the British troops. Besides these and the profiteering shopkeepers, there was quite a number of very friendly French ladies, but they gradually disappeared before the big offensive started, although some of the less obvious kind remained throughout, especially those who had—or conveniently adopted—aged parents to take care of. The old folks didn't seem to mind much. Often the old grandpere would sit cackling with laughter in a corner while he listened to the troops singing the usual ribald songs such as " Apris la guerre fini." However, our military police were fairly adept at keeping a control over that sort of thing, perhaps because so many of that type were spies. Once they were marked down by the " red-caps " they were soon removed from the British army area.

The French civilians as a rule were not much in evidence in the daytime, but during a prolonged quiet spell, when there had been no serious bombardment for a day or two, they would venture out more freely, and occasionally in the quieter districts a few children would even be seen playing about the streets. If shells came over anywhere in the neighbourhood there would be screams of " a la cave, a la cave! " and back they would scuttle to their underground cellars. I have seen an elderly French civilian, neatly dressed in black overcoat, bowler hat and gloves, carrying his umbrella and a net market bag for his morning shopping, placidly crossing the Station Place; a dangerous open space that was constantly swept by high-angle machine-gun fire from the German trenches.

Although Arras was full of troops, they were not

allowed to leave their billets during the day except on duty, and with the deserted streets and shuttered shops the place in daytime seemed a city of the dead. But many of the shops, although kept closely shuttered, were nevertheless open for business, and our mess cook sometimes was even able to buy fresh fish that had been brought in overnight. Every morning the Paris edition of the *Daily Mail* was to be obtained from the newsagent round the corner. The same newspaper shop seemed to do a roaring trade in picture postcards with the troops when they were allowed out of billets after dark. However, the last time I saw that shop it was a heap of ruins, as was the whole of the block of buildings of which it formed part. There were also a theatre, and a hotel that functioned right up until the big push commenced in April, and no doubt they have carried on since that stormy period without a break. In the hotel (the Hotel de Commerce) one could have quite a good dinner in the evening, served by waitresses and paid for to a girl clerk in the cash desk ; in fact, we company commanders of the 12th H.L.I. had dinner there with our commanding officer on the evening of the 8th of April, the night before the big attack.

The theatre was used for holding Divisional concert parties, and very good they were as a rule, the best talent of the whole division being specially collected for that purpose. Some evenings the building was as crammed full of British troops as ever it could have been with a civilian audience in its pre-war days. An air-bomb or two dropped on that theatre at these times would have made a shocking mess.

A remarkable feature of Arras is the number and size of the cellars with which the city is honeycombed underground. Most of the houses have a big cellar underneath, some of them enormous caverns with well-built vaulted roofs, and they are usually reached by a steep flight of stairs leading from the street pavement at the front of the house. What these great cellars were originally constructed for is a mystery, but no doubt they had some use ; perhaps as storage warehouses in the days when Arras was one of the great commercial centres of Europe. I think it very probable that the soft white limestone of which Arras is built was quarried on the site of the city, and the cavities from which it was taken afterwards converted into these cellars. Anyhow, they provided safe accommodation for a great number of troops, and maybe that is why Arras was chosen as the centre for the big operations in the Spring of 1917.

CHAPTER XXX

THE OLD FRENCH FRONT AT ARRAS

OUR first spell of front-line duty at Arras was comparatively uneventful. We found the trenches well constructed and fairly dry, with plenty of good dugouts and other cover, and—what had become something of a novelty for us—the entrances to the dugouts all faced the right way, that is *away* from the enemy. There had been no movement to speak of in that part of the front since early in 1915, and during that long spell of sedentary warfare, while the French and Germans were sitting down making faces at each other, the defence systems on both sides had been elaborately developed. On our side, the city of Arras itself was fortified by barricades of paving stones or barbed wire across the main thoroughfares, and in all the streets on the eastern side. Some of the communication trenches to the front line actually commenced in these streets, in which they looked like the familiar excavations made in our streets at home for the laying of drains and waterpipes. Starting in these communication trenches there was good cover all the way to the front line, and reliefs were regularly carried out in the daytime, without all the discomfort and dirty work we had latterly been accustomed to on the Somme, where reliefs could only be effected after a laborious and dangerous night march across the open.

The section of front taken over by the 15th Division was directly in front of the city, running from the banks of the River Scarpe on the left to east of the cemetery, a stretch of about a thousand yards or so. No-man's land was fairly wide, except on the left where the trenches cut right through the ruined houses and factories of Blangy village, and there in some places not more than fifteen or twenty yards separated the enemy trenches from our own. At one point we could look down into the German front trench from an observation hole in the wall of a ruined factory we called the " Boiler House." In that dangerous neighbourhood great caution had to be taken in traversing the front trench, which was well within bomb-slinging distance of the enemy. He, of course, found it just as unhealthy. To avoid unnecessary casualties where the opposing trenches were in such close proximity they were not fully garrisoned on either side, but occupied only by an occasional sentry or listening-post.

It was at the " Boiler House " one morning that a man of the 10th Scottish Rifles captured a German prisoner, in rather a unique fashion. While having a look through the observation hole in the factory wall he spotted a German sentry lounging in the opposite trench, apparently indulging in a daydream. Descending from the wall the rifleman sprinted across and hurled a Mill's bomb at the surprised German, who tried to bolt. As it happened, the Scot in the excitement of the moment forgot to pull out the pin that releases the spring in the bomb, but by a lucky chance the " dud " bomb hit the German a crack on the head, and the result was nearly as effective as if it had been a " live " one. Anyhow, the dazed German quietly accompanied his captor back to the British trench without any more to do. The pound-and-a-half of knobbly serrated cast iron that forms the shell of a Mill's bomb is in itself a very useful missile if it hits the mark.

As I have said, the sector was a fairly quiet one at the time we took it over, although the enemy occasionally put in some effective artillery practice, which was directed on our support trenches as much as on the front line, and particularly on the communication trenches to the rear. The communication trenches were deep and well traversed, but some of them had the defect of running back from the front in too direct a line, and these long straight furrows of upturned chalk must have presented easy targets for the German artillery observers on the higher ground to the east. Certainly he seemed to have them all well marked down, and he did not let us forget it when he felt in an aggressive mood.

How thorough the enemy's knowledge of our trenches was I saw for myself a few weeks later, when we broke through his front line and over his artillery positions. In a German artillery dugout I saw a large map of the city of Arras, showing all our defences and trenches in as complete detail as if it had been one of our own maps for staff use. On it lines were drawn giving the direction and distance in metres from that particular battery position to every trench and point of importance in our defence system. If all their batteries were provided with similar maps, as was doubtless the case, it is not to be wondered at that they could concentrate such heavy fire at short notice on any particular part of our line when occasion required, as they often did. However, I don't think our own artillery were one whit behind them in that respect, nor were our maps of their trenches and positions any less accurate. At any rate, we had the opportunity of verifying our maps when later we went over in force for a '' look see,'' whereas the Germans never at any time up till the end of the war set foot over our old front line in the Arras sector.

With the deep dugouts and other good cover in our front line, the enemy artillery did not bother us too much, at least, not so much as it did in the support area, but in this sector we found he made a speciality of a light trench mortar which fired a bomb known to us as a ''pineapple'' or ''fish tail.'' It had a serrated body about the size and shape of a pineapple, and a flanged tail like a fish, hence the obvious names we gave it. Ordinary artillery shells we were used to and could make allowances for, because they could be heard in the air, and we were able to judge fairly accurately from experience the direction they were travelling and where they were likely to land, but these light trench mortar bombs came over with a sudden swish without any warning. They were nasty little brutes, and they caused us a number of casualties at first.

Another weapon frequently used by the enemy in that sector when we took over was the rifle grenade, a weapon of which we had not had much experience hitherto. We had our own British rifle grenade, of course ; the Hales No. 1, but up till then we had not made a great deal of use of it, perhaps because the conditions to which we had become accustomed to on the Somme were not much suited to its employment. That it could be a deadly weapon in settled trench warfare, however, we very soon learnt from the Germans ; in fact, on our first day in the Arras trenches a man of my company had half his head blown away by an enemy rifle grenade. He was peering up into a little mirror periscope he had fixed on the trench parados, when the grenade burst right in front of his face. We were not going to put up quietly with that sort of thing, of course, and we took immediate steps to give the Boche a taste of his own medicine. In a neglected support trench I found some old rusty fixed-rifle stands, one of which I had conveyed up to the head of a sap running out in front of our trenches. Taking advantage of some shelling that was going on, so as not to arouse the enemy's suspicions, we did a little practice with a fixed rifle clamped to the stand until we had got the exact range of the German sap from which we knew their rifle grenades mostly came. That evening after " stand to," when we knew the opposing sap was certain to be occupied, we let off three grenades in quick succession, and judging by the shrieks and commotion that arose from the German trench it was apparent we had scored a hit. All their other saps and listening posts within range were subjected in due course to the same attention, and from then on I think the Boche rather regretted that he had shown us what could be done with rifle grenades.

CHAPTER XXXI

Sudden Death in the Trenches

For the next few weeks, that is, until our big offensive started early in April, we settled down to the usual sedentary trench warfare, and there is nothing of much interest to record during that period. At first things were rather quiet, and sometimes a whole day would pass without incident, but as time went on the war gradually livened up, as the Germans became aware of the preparations that were going ahead behind our lines, and of the masses of artillery being pushed into Arras and the neighbourhood.

At this time several raids on the enemy trenches were carried out by our brigade and the other brigades of the division. We hated those raids, which were always made at night under the most difficult conditions. Ostensibly the object was to capture prisoners for the purpose of obtaining information regarding enemy reliefs and the movement of troops behind his lines, and if we could not bring back live prisoners we brought their shoulder-straps showing the regiment they belonged to, also any papers they might have on them. I still have a collection of these German shoulder-straps in my possession. Almost invariably these night raids cost us more in casualties than the results warranted. However, I suppose it was part of the policy of our staff to harass the enemy as much as possible and to keep him on the jump. The lives of infantrymen were cheap at that time. I was told once by an officer attached to a H.Q. staff of two brigadier-generals who, having dined well in the headquarters mess far behind the lines, made a bet over the port as to whose brigade would capture most prisoners in a trench raid competition !

The enemy meanwhile must have been well aware of the impending big attack, and he was bringing up new divisions and strong reinforcements of artillery to cope with it. That was apparent from the increasing frequency of his bombardments, and the incessant ranging practice carried out by his newly arrived batteries on all our positions. It was in one of these bombardments that Porter, my batman, was killed. My company that afternoon had just been relieved in the front line and had gone back a few hundred yards to the support trenches. The second-in-command, Lieut. McLean, and I had remained behind to complete the handing over, and it was while we were making our way back along the communication trench to rejoin the company, accompanied by our batmen, Porter and Thompson, that the shelling started. The two batmen were going on in front, and they had just preceded us around a traverse into a long straight bay of the trench, when a 77mm shell (a " whizz-bang ") skimmed close over our heads and blew them both to bits. Incredible as it may seem, when we saw the ghastly mess in the trench we could not tell at first whether only one or both men had been killed. They were literally torn to shreds. That poor Porter was killed was only too evident, for his head lay there with only a fragment of quivering naked breast attached to it. The sight of that blood-bespattered waxen face staring up at me is still a vivid memory. And yet, only a few seconds before, these dreadful remains that now lay strewn about the blown-in-trench, from which the fumes of the shell had scarcely cleared, had been two men full of life and health, laughing and joking with one another. However, such is war.

CHAPTER XXXII

THE RESERVE AREA

IN these weeks the three brigades of our division took turns of front line duty in rotation ; one brigade being in the trenches while the other two were in divisional support and reserve. The reserve area of our Corps (rest billets it was sometimes called) was in the district ten to fifteen kilometers behind the front line, in the angle formed by the main roads from Arras to St. Pol and Doullens, and the first part of the march back was always made by night, for the reason that it was impossible to march out of Arras during the daytime. As I mentioned before, the roads out of the city were well under enemy observation, and all movement of bodies of troops on them in daylight was prohibited. Night marches are always tiresome, but when we had our pipers with us it seemed to make the distance shorter. Sometimes on passing through a village in the dead of night our pipes and drums would strike up a rousing march, such as the " Black Bear," and it was cheering to see the lights appear at the windows and the French folk flock to the doorways to see what the commotion was about. Even English troops billetted in these villages would leave their warm straw in the barns and come out to watch us pass. On the long stretches of road between the villages, however, the pipers were usually as tired as the rest of us, although they never did any trench work. Their special and rather expensive uniforms were purchased out of our Officers' Mess fund, and therefore we never risked them too near the firing line !

It must not be thought that arrival in " rest billets " meant nothing but a rest for us, or that the men were allowed to idle away the time while we were back in the support area. Leisure they had in the afternoons for games and sports, but most of the day was taken up in hard training and the many routine duties that make up a solider's day. The officers also were kept busy. On arrival at the destination for the night, the platoon commanders had to see that their men were properly billetted and made as comfortable as circumstances permitted, before they could repair to their own quarters. The company commander made a final inspection of all his company's billets; saw that the field kitchens were housed and a hot meal prepared for the men; received the sergeant-major's report and issued orders for the next day, and generally was kept pretty well occupied for a while. Sometimes on getting into billets in the early hours of the morning I was not able to get to bed at all that night. Perhaps that is why infantry company commanders are provided with horses, so that after a march they may arrive fresh for the multitude of routine duties that await them. First thing in the morning after a march, a foot inspection for the men was held. Care of the feet is a first essential in the infantry, and great importance was attached to these foot inspections, which were carried out frequently.

A job that took up a good part of the officers' spare time, in the trenches as well as in billets, was the censoring of the men's letters. It was strictly against regulations for anyone in their letters home to touch on the subject of morale, or to say anything about the situation or movements of their units. And on these points some letters badly called for censoring. These army censorship regulations were undoubtedly wise, because a lot of useful information might have got through to the enemy if everyone had been allowed to write freely about the movements of our divisions; to say nothing of the anxiety and distress that might have been caused at home to the relatives of " windy " soldiers. This censoring of letters was no small job, and it was astonishing the subterfuges some men would invent, although they well knew they were risking severe punishment, to get through forbidden information to their friends at home. I have seen some letters re-enveloped after the censorship consisting only of the opening " Dear Mother " —with the usual tail end part pinned on —" Hoping you are well as this leaves me at present," the whole body of the letter having been cut out. That drastic treatment was not done unless absolutely necessary, of course. While we were on the Somme front it was common for men to write in their letters " This is *somme* show," or to endeavour by suchlike play on the word " some " to convey the news that they were on the Somme to their anxious relatives, who no doubt would not be relieved to know it. A more subtle dodge to pass on secret messages was to make tiny pinholes beneath certain letters. That was easily spotted by holding the letter up to the light, and we merely made a lot more pinholes all over the page so as to obscure the message.

Apart from the stoppage of information, however, the censoring of letters gave us a fine insight into the mentality of the men under our command. The sentiments expressed in some of them were crude in the extreme, and I have seen letters to wives and sweethearts that were downright shocking in what one might call their lack of finesse. The writers believed in calling a spade a spade, without any attempt at delicacy of language ! However, we didn't stop these, because they probably cheered up some lonely female hearts at home, and in any case it was no business of ours. On the other hand, there were letters written by educated men, and by some not so educated, that were really fine and worthy of preservation by their recipients.

Although it was a serious offence for a man to contravene the censorship regulations, we very seldom ran them up for it ; we rectified it in our own way. Only on one occasion did I have a man brought up for that offence. He was a recently " returned wounded " who had previously served in the 9th Division, and in his letter to a friend he bitterly lamented (like a good soldier) that he had not been returned to his own original unit, instead of which, he wrote, he had been drafted to " this bloody mealy-mouthed . . . mob ! " That was too much !

One thing we always looked forward to when going back to the divisional support and reserve areas was the opportunity of indulging in a proper bath—of which we were usually badly in need after a spell of duty in the front line. While in the trenches our clothes were never taken off for days on end, though in the ordinary way things were seldom so bad that we could not manage to have a wash with a shave and brush-up daily. Behind the lines, however, there were divisional bathhouses to which the men were taken regularly for a hot bath and a complete change of underclothing. The discarded clothing was all sent to be dealt with at the divisional " de-lousing " centre. Sometimes these army bath-houses consisted only of a few canvas screens out in the fields and quite open to all weathers—somewhat chilly in the winter, perhaps, but there was always plenty of hot water and soap, and they served their purpose very well. The men had to herd themselves in and wash all together out of troughs. Often the divisional bath-houses were at an inconvenient distance, but we could always have a bath in the backyard of our billet as often as we wished. I remember one afternoon bathing myself behind an outhouse at the back of the small farm-house where we were billetted ; the bathing being done out of a bucket of hot water placed on top of what I thought was an empty box. While I was busy lathering myself Madame appeared, and, apologising politely, but without a blush, she removed my bucket and lifted the lid of the box, from which she withdrew by the ears a struggling rabbit, which she proceeded to slaughter on the spot for the family supper. The French country people seemed to think nothing of that sort of thing. When we were on the Somme front, on those few occa-sions when we could get back to Amiens, our first visit was always to the municipal baths to indulge in the

I

luxury of wallowing at our leisure in clean and un-
limited hot water. The establishment we patronised
was a big one and fairly well appointed, but none of the
cubicles appeared to have locks on the doors, and all the
bath attendants were females, even in the '' Hommes ''
section.   One was not expected to be startled if madame
(known to us as '' Old Mother Judge '') came barging in,
without so much as a knock at the door, to inquire
whether one had plenty of soap, although she herself
had probably just handed out soap and a towel when
allotting the cubicle.

On one occasion in the support trenches on the
Somme, when we were expecting to be withdrawn to
reserve but suddenly received orders to return to the
front line, another officer and I had a midnight bath in a
big shell hole.   The stagnant water was frozen and
filthy, and I am afraid that after slithering about in that
odoriferous mud we emerged rather dirtier than before,
but at any rate it was a change of dirt.   Getting our
underclothing washed was often another difficulty in the
depth of winter.   The clothes, when hung out in the
open, would not dry, and sometimes we were forced to
put on a change of under-garments while they were still
frozen stiff, and allow them to thaw on our bodies.

CHAPTER XXXIII

Preparations for the Offensive

On our last spell back in the Divisional reserve area we were put through special training for the forthcoming big operations. An extensive stretch of the countryside had been taken over by the British H.Q. Staff for that purpose, and this special training ground was laid out with shallow furrows representing to scale all the trenches and strong points in that part of the German front that would form the objective of our division. These practices over this prepared ground, which were carried out by us in the extended formation and at the same rate of advance that was to be employed in the actual attack, gave us a more comprehensive idea of the general lay-out of the enemy system of defences than could have been obtained from the study of maps alone, and it proved very useful to us later on. The preparations made by our General Staff for the Arras offensive, which included this preliminary training for the infantry, were certainly very thorough.

After being refitted and receiving a draft of reinforcements, which, however, did not bring us up to anything like full strength, we moved back to the front towards the end of March. On this occasion we did not enter Arras by the main road as usual, but by a circuitous route that took us round by the River Scarpe and the outlying village of St. Nicholas, thence into the city by the north side. Our march was timed so that we should approach Arras after dark, and it was while we were halted at a point on the road some distance from the city, waiting for dusk to fall, that something of a disaster befell a detachment of Marine Artillerymen in that locality. Near where we had fallen out, two very large naval guns on railway mountings were being worked by these men, and on the other side of the road were some corrugated iron huts that apparently formed the living quarters of the detachment. As we sat by the roadside watching the artillerymen at work, and fascinated by the terrific reports of the big guns as they fired, a heavy German shell came over and made a direct hit on one of the huts behind us, killing and wounding nearly a score of the Marines. It was just an unlucky chance that that particular hut happened to be full of men at the time.

After a few days in Arras in brigade reserve, we took over the right half of our divisional front, which was now held by two battalions. The time spent in reserve, although we were quartered in houses and cellars in the middle of the city, was rather a busy one for us, all companies being kept well occupied during the day and a good part of each night in fatigues and working parties. There were also lectures for the senior officers and company commanders at Divisional H.Q. on the forthcoming operations, at which full and detailed instructions were given regarding the part to be played by each unit. Up till then, of course, we were still unaware of the actual date on which the big attack was to take place, but the general programme and time-table were carefully explained to us ; the time-table for the capture of each objective being in the usual form of '' zero plus so-many hours,'' as was always adopted in these shows. The '' zero hour,'' that is, the actual starting time for the attack, was kept secret until the evening before we went over.

At one of these lectures I remember we saw a large plaster-cast map which showed in relief the contours of the terrain beyond the enemy front line. A close study of this model enabled me to memorise the main features and landmarks, and especially the directions followed by the ridges and declivities of the ground we were to advance over ; a knowledge that stood us in good stead during the actual show. The ability to keep direction is always of the utmost importance, even in minor operations such as trench raids, if they are to penetrate any distance within the enemy lines, and although it may perhaps be thought an easy matter to advance in a straight line during an attack, in practice it is not so simple as it seems. Without any conspicuous landmarks the enemy trenches all look very much alike, and where the ground is undulating the tendency is always to advance directly up the face of a slope instead of diagonally towards an allotted objective as may be required. Failure to keep direction, by units veering too much to the right or left, results in pockets of enemy machine gunners and snipers being left in parts, which delays the advance, and may perhaps jeopardise the success of the whole operations. Time after time this happened in all the big pushes, and even in the Arras battle, despite the very thorough preliminary training, there were battalions and even whole brigades that lost direction, with serious results to themselves and the units on their flanks.

Our last tour of duty in the old front line trenches in that sector passed without incident and with only a few casualties. During the night before we were relieved we cut all the barbed wire in front of our line ; a night's work that left us with many lacerated hands and torn uniforms, the old wire being rusty and thickly massed. Whether the Boche noticed at the time that we had destroyed our own barbed wire defences I cannot say, but maybe at the moment he had all his time taken up in repairing his own wire, which was then being incessantly shelled by our artillery and trench mortars. From the front line we were withdrawn to support, where we spent the remaining two or three days before the big push in underground cellars in the neighbourhood of the Grand Place, or " Barbed-Wire Square " as we called it, because the whole centre of the fine old market place was blocked by barbed wire entanglements left by the French.

Arras by this time seemed to be full of artillery ; there were guns of all sorts in every position within the city that allowed a field of fire, and howitzers were blazing away in the most unexpected places, such as the back-yards of houses, and even in the grounds of the Bishop's palace. The clamour at times was deafening. The enemy in the meantime was not remaining idle, and he vigorously bombarded Arras day and night with high explosive and shrapnel, and especially with gas shells, of which he must have put over a great number, though I don't think they did very much harm. However, in our snug underground retreats we were not bothered a great deal by all this racket, which reached us only as a continuous series of overhead thumps, punctuated every now and then by heavier thumps as enemy high ex-plosive shells landed in our near vicinity ; sometimes heavy enough to shake the mortar from the roofs of our old cellars, and to make us think they were about to cave in. At any rate, these big cellars were vastly superior to any trench dugouts we had known, and we contrived to make ourselves fairly comfortable in them, although the troglodyte existence we were forced to lead began to pall on us after the first day or so. Day and night were much the same to us living by candlelight underground. No troops were allowed out of their billets except on duty, and we officers were at our wits end in devising means to keep the men occupied and help them fill in the time during these long hours of inactive waiting. Kit and foot inspections, with an occasional lecture, were about as much as our efforts in that direction could amount to after the first twenty-four hours, although there was still some final equipping to be done that pro-vided us with some occupation. Fitting out an in-fantryman to go over the top nowadays is like loading a pack mule. There seems no end to the kag he has to carry.

Although the men were not allowed out of those stuffy cellars during the day, they were taken out for fresh air and exercise after nightfall, as was of course ab-solutely necessary. With the intensive shelling then going on, it was a risky business for large bodies of men to move about in the streets even after dark, but in our battalion no orders were laid down as to the routes we were to follow on these outings, and each company commander was left to take his men wherever he thought best. They mustered in the cellars lightly armed, that is, carrying only a slung rifle and a canvas bandolier of ammunition, and on emerging up to the streets from our subterranean lodgings we moved quietly in single file round the leeward side of " Barbed-wire Square," then the most shelled part of Arras, and from there proceeded on our constitutional. On each occasion I led my company at a smart double down through the more or less open industrial area on the banks of the river, which was in full view of the enemy from the Vimy Ridge side in the daytime, and we were quite unmolested. It often happens in war that the closer you get to the enemy the safer it is.

Those three days in the cellars under Arras were not so boring for the officers as for the men. Final operation orders had now been issued, and we officers were out part of the time reconnoitring the routes we would follow in moving up from our underground billets in the centre of the city and deploying over the top when we reached the open. As may well be imagined, it required a very finely adjusted time table to ensure that the great number of troops concentrated in the city and its neighbourhood, all at various distances from the front line, which each unit would reach by a different route to avoid congestion, should gain their allotted sections of the front in time to move forward simultaneously to the attack in their proper formation. That the first phase of the operations subsequently passed off so well says a lot for the work of our H.Q. Staff. In our own case, the route arranged for us was by a passage that had been constructed by the R.E. through the maze of underground caverns to one of the main city sewers, which we followed for some distance until we reached a long steep flight of dugout stairs that brought us up to the open air in the centre of a ruined factory on the north-east outskirts of the city. From there, each unit made its own way by a previously reconnoitred route to its section of the attacking line. All this was well organised, our divisional engineers having even put up direction signboards in all the passages between the cellars and installed electric light along the big sewer.

While we were living in those cellars awaiting the commencement of the push our commanding officer gave a dinner to the company commanders in the Hotel de Commerce, which was still carrying on business as usual, although the upper stories were completely wrecked, and the back part just a mass of ruins.

The night before the attack being Easter Sunday (8th April, 1917) a church service was held in the largest of the cellars by our padre (Father Steuart), and although it was voluntary I noticed it was fully attended by the men. Another officer and I squatted smoking our pipes at the top of the stone stairs watching the impressive scene in the great crowded cavern below, which was illuminated only by candles stuck in brackets around the walls. It was always noticeable how religious many men became when death was looming ahead, but unfortunately in most cases the mood only lasted as long as the danger. That same night I remember a young officer of " C " Company, who had recently joined us, spent a good part of the night in praying, regardless of our repeated shouts on him to turn in and get some rest. Perhaps the lad had a premonition that something was to happen to him, and if so, it was true, for he died with a bullet through the throat early next day.

CHAPTER XXXIV

The Big Push

THE offensive by the British Third Army (General Allenby) was launched on 9th April at the zero hour of 5-30 a.m. On our divisional front (the 15th Scottish Division), the attack was led by the 44th Brigade on the right and the 45th Brigade on the left, while on our right flank was the 12th Division, and on the left, on the other side of the River Scarpe, the 9th Division. In the opening phase of the attack, our 44th and 45th Brigades had for their first objective the German front line with its immediate support trenches (designated in Operation Orders the " Black Line "), and for their second objective the rising ground about fifteen hundred yards beyond, known as " Observation Ridge " (the " Blue Line "). The task allotted to our own brigade, the 46th, was to follow in support of the other two brigades, and after the capture and consolidation by them of the first two objectives, to pass through them to the capture of a third objective, Himalaya Trench (the " Brown Line ") a very strong trench system on the slope of Orange Hill at a distance of over two miles behind the enemy front line. Himalaya Trench was in fact part of the strong German secondary line of defence better known later as the Hindenburg Line.

Zero hour was 5-30 a.m. as I have said, but it was earlier than that when we commenced to move from the cellars to the front. The first part of our subterranean journey was very slow, as we could only proceed in single file through the narrow and tortuous passages that had been constructed from cellar to cellar, but when we reached the main sewer the going was easier, though still slow and in single file. Many jokes were passed

among the men as we made our way along that salu-
brious emergency thoroughfare. In the good old days,
troops went into battle with colours flying and bands
playing, but there is not much romance in advancing to
the attack through a city sewer !

However, we eventually reached the long flight of dugout stairs that took us up to the fresh air. When we
emerged among the factory ruins above, it was still
rather dark and raining, and as the attack was now well
started the din of the guns had reached crescendo, though
not many enemy shells were coming over our way.
From there we proceeded for some distance along an old
communication trench ; then we crossed the railway
cutting, the steep muddy banks of which presented
rather a difficult obstacle for our heavily laden men ;
and so on through the streets of the Fauberge on the
other side to the cemetery, through which we passed by
a fine new communication trench that had been constructed a few weeks before by our own pioneer battalion,
the 9th Gordons. The yellow skulls of many former
citizens of Arras grinned at us from the walls and heaped-
up parapets of that trench as we pushed our way by.

So far we had suffered no casualties, and it was not
till we were winding through the streets of the Fauberge
that we saw the first dead man that day ; an English
infantryman who had just been killed by shrapnel. He
lay sprawling across the sidewalk, with a rivulet of blood
running to the pavement kerb. Some of the reinforce-
ment draft that had recently joined us were fresh conscripts, and as we filed past the dead man I glanced back
to observe how these new lads took the sight. One or
two of them were making forced jokes, but others
sheered round the corpse with white faces and sidelong
glances, as if it was something to be avoided.

On clearing the cemetery, we left the communication
trench and extended over the open in " artillery formation," that is, in line of platoons in single file columns at
wide intervals. In that order we continued the advance
across our own and the German front line trenches

into his support area, which by this time had been captured by the 44th Brigade in front of us. While getting over that open ground, however, a distance of more than a thousand yards, we had a bad gruelling, for the enemy artillery just then laid down a fierce barrage that caused us a large number of casualties. In that short space of time, even at this early stage before our own part in the attack had commenced in earnest, our casualties included half the company signallers and stretcher bearers, the men we could least afford to lose. From the intensity of the enemy barrage, and the promptness with which it opened on us as we emerged to the open ground, it was obvious that the 44th and 45th Brigades had not yet succeeded in penetrating to their second objective on Observation Ridge, where the Germans must still have had observers directing their artillery fire on us.

Apart from the hot barrage just mentioned, we encountered practically no opposition at this stage, although we found several pockets of Germans in shell holes and side trenches that had been overlooked by the troops that went over before us. In this way we pushed on to the main support trench of the enemy front defences, a thickly wired trench named in our maps Hermes Trench (the " Black Line "), which according to Operation Orders was our assembly point for the second phase of the operations, that is, for our long two mile advance against the formidable Himalaya Trench and Orange Hill.

Here in Hermes and the adjacent trenches we had a lengthy wait until the scheduled hour for the continuation of the attack ; the time of waiting being spent by us in reorganising our forces, which had become somewhat mixed up, and in putting in some consolidation work on the position ; also in searching around the trenches and clearing the dugouts. This enemy support trench was a very deep one, much deeper than any German trenches we had seen on the Somme, and from the strength of its construction it seemed to have been intended as the main line of defence in the enemy front system. Like all the other trenches we had passed over so far that morning, it was badly damaged by our artillery preparation for the attack, which, as was evident also by the number of dead and wounded Germans lying about, had been very thoroughly carried out.

Some of the German wounded we sent back to our own lines in care of prisoners that were routed out from the dugouts, and whom we utilised as emergency stretcher bearers, so many of our own stretcher bearers having become casualties themselves, but I am afraid a good number of the more seriously wounded died from lack of prompt surgical attention, although we did what we could for them with the means at our disposal. As usual in the case of high explosive artillery fire, the wounds were mostly rather ghastly; I remember one young German soldier there who had been disembowelled by a shell splinter. He was lying on a fire step with his intestines looped up in a bag formed by his undershirt pulled over them, and as we moved about in the trench he eyed us with an air of mild interest, as if we were the first British soldiers he had ever seen. Of course, he and others in a like condition, of whom there were many, were beyond our help, even had there been a sufficient number of stretcher bearers left with us to attend and evacuate the enemy wounded as well as our own. The man who was wounded at an early stage in these shows was fortunate, for there was a chance of him getting quickly back to a dressing station, whereas the hope of being safely evacuated diminished the farther an advance progressed beyond our own lines.

In our search through the dugouts in these trenches we found many things of interest, besides a number of live Germans who were still taking refuge in them. In one big dugout, which seemed to be a Battalion or Company Headquarters, the occupants had evidently been in the custom of doing themselves well, judging by the number of empty bottles lying about. Amongst these we discovered one or two full bottles of cognac and '' rhum '' which of course we promptly '' salved,'' as well as a large quantity of cigars of the usual German "army issue" kind. Our commanding officer joined us as I was squatting outside that dugout in the midst of several dead Germans, writing a situation report and smoking one of these cigars, as were most of our men in the vicinity at the time, and I think he rather disapproved of this general cigar smoking during business hours as rather unsoldierlike !

CHAPTER XXXV

THE ATTACK PROCEEDS

WE resumed the attack simultaneously with the 12th Division on our right, according to the pre-arranged time-table, at, I think, 11 a.m. Our advance on this occasion, as already mentioned, was to be a non-stop one against the third objective consisting of the German back system of defences, Himalaya Trench and Orange Hill, to reach which we would pass through the 44th and 45th Brigades in front of us, which by this time should have captured and well consolidated the second objective. We had no sooner got going over the top, however, than machine gun and rifle fire opened on us from several parts of Observation Ridge, and especially from the Hart Work, an enemy strong point two or three hundred yards on our half right. It was at once evident that our 44th Brigade had failed to capture the second objective, or at any rate the right-hand part of it. As a matter of fact, from then on for the rest of the day we saw practically no men of the 44th Brigade, from which it would seem that that brigade had veered too far to the left in their advance during the morning, thus leaving a considerable gap on the ridge that was still fairly strongly held by the enemy.

Before we had proceeded any distance, the enemy fire became so hot that our attack was held up, and we were forced to take cover in shell holes and in the remains of an old support trench, while on the right the 12th Division likewise were brought to a standstill. The situation for us was untenable. Practically the whole battalion was packed into that old trench, which being shallow and in many places almost levelled by shell fire, afforded very little cover, crowded with men as it was. To remain where we were was out of the question, as it was only a matter of time before the enemy artillery would grasp the situation and concentrate fire on the trench, and when that happened nothing was more certain than that we should be pounded out of existence. As it was, the German machine gunners and snipers were taking their toll of us, and it was plain that our only course was to push on. I therefore suggested to the Commanding Officer (who, with his H.Q. had followed our advance to that point) that I should lead forward my company in widely extended formation to test the real enemy strength, to which proposal he acquiesced, though rather doubtfully.

It is extraordinary how even in such times of confusion and turmoil little incidents stick clearly in one's memory long after other things are forgotten. Among the victims that fell to the German riflemen just then was a young lad in McLean's platoon ; I think he was one of our remaining bantams. He was only a boy, obviously not more than about seventeen years of age, but he had always refused to be sent back to the Base Depot along with the other '' under-ages.'' The bullet struck him in the belly, and as usual in the case of these abdominal wounds he rolled about clawing the ground, screaming and making a terrible fuss. Certainly, to have one's guts stirred up by a red-hot bullet must be a dreadful thing, and that a bullet is really hot after its flight through the air is well known to anyone who has tried to pick up a newly spent one. However, they got the boy back into the trench, opened his clothes and put a bandage around his middle over the wound, but of course we could see from the first it was hopeless. A little later, as I was squeezing my way along the crowded trench passing the word to '' A '' Company to be ready to go over on the signal, I noticed the lad laid out on a blown-in part of the trench. By then he was lying very still, and I thought he was dead, but as I passed he half opened his eyes and said something to me. I had to stoop down to catch what he said ; it was '' Good luck to you, sir ! ''

When I gave the signal for " A " Company to lead on, not only " A " Company, but the whole battalion as well went over, and the 12th Division on our right also joined in the advance, which thus became a general one all along the line instead of merely a single company reconnaissance in force as intended ! The advance was made without any covering barrage from our own artillery, but as we approached the crest of the ridge the enemy fire slackened, and the position was taken with less difficulty and fewer losses than we anticipated. A number of the Germans managed to make their escape down the trenches on the reverse slope of the ridge, and the remainder we dealt with.   One cannot but have admiration for an enemy machine gunner or sniper who sticks to his post till the last, that is, if he fully realises he has no chance of escape ; but the enemy who continues to deal death and wounds to advancing troops from his own comparatively safe shelter until they are almost on him, in the expectation that when unable to carry on that work any longer he has only to put up his hands and surrender, has no cause for complaint if things do not turn out for him quite as he expected.

Something of a surprise awaited us as we pushed on over the crest of Observation Ridge, for there on the reverse slope, not more than two to three hundred yards directly in front of us, were two batteries of German field guns that opened point-blank fire on us as soon as we appeared in view. It was something new and certainly very uncomfortable to find ourselves so close up to the muzzles of enemy guns in action ; the range was so short that the flash of the guns and the explosion of the shells amongst our men seemed instantaneous. We were in extended formation, of course, but in the few minutes we were under that deadly fire several men were killed and a number terribly wounded. I remember catching a glimpse of my new batman, Don, with a gash in his neck that looked as if his head were almost severed, and beside him, standing stockstill in his tracks and looking at me in a helpless sort of fashion, as if he wanted to know what I was going to do about it, was our mess cook with a spurting red mass of flesh on his shoulder where his arm had been. For the second time that day—and we had to decide quickly this time—we found our safest direction lay right ahead ; in fact our only course in that situation was to rush the guns, which we did. We " ca'ed the feet from them," as our Clydesiders put it, and I think we got most of the Boche artillerymen, including at least one battery officer, whose spurs and shoulder-straps are still in my possession. They belonged to the 42nd Field Artillery Regiment.

After silencing the German batteries, we moved on across the narrow valley named in our maps " Battery Valley " (for very obvious reasons, as we had just discovered !), but we had scarcely commenced the ascent of the opposite slope than a runner from Battalion Headquarters overtook us with a message that our artillery was about to open a covering barrage for our advance from a line running approximately along the bottom of the valley. We had already got beyond that point, but as there was no sense in remaining to be pounded by our own artillery we retired a few hundred yards to behind the promised barrage line. We had not long to wait, in fact we had scarcely cleared the arranged line before the barrage opened and we turned to resume the advance. Our " B " Company I noticed did not retire far enough, and for some distance they went on right under our own artillery fire, which apparently they mistook for enemy shelling ! However, the covering barrage, although no doubt meant with the best of intentions by our gunners, was very scrappy, we having now advanced to beyond effective range from our field artillery positions, and before we had gone much farther it fizzled out and was lost altogether. In any case it was unnecessary, as there were no enemy defences worth mentioning between where we then were and our third and main objective.

On reaching the crest of the opposite side of Battery Valley we got our first view of that objective, Himalaya

K

Trench, about a thousand yards away on the slope of Orange Hill. It certainly looked formidable, with immensely thick belts of bristling barbed wire in front of it. The Boche also got his first view of us just then, for his machine guns began to chatter at us as soon as we appeared over the crest of the ridge.   However, at that moment we were cheered by the sight of one of our tanks (the first and only one we saw that day) crawling along the front of Himalaya Trench from the direction of Feuchy Village on the left, and vigorously using its guns against the enemy machine gun emplacements. The tank did not get very far before it was brought to a standstill by a well directed enemy shell, but it was wonderful the confidence these mechanical monsters inspired in us infantrymen, and we pushed on across the intervening ground with all the haste our heavily laden men could make.

CHAPTER XXXVI

CAPTURE OF A STRONG POSITION.

As we advanced over that long stretch of open ground machine guns opened on us from all points in front, and the German snipers also made the best practice they could, but as we were in widely extended formation and our numbers were already woefully thin, they did not make so much execution among us as might be thought. I think myself that the machine gun, although undoubtedly an extremely useful weapon in warfare, is often overrated. Its burst of fire of ten to twenty bullets either hits the one mark or is wasted on the empty ground, whereas the distributed fire of a section of fifteen well trained independent riflemen is much more likely to hit several marks. Nevertheless, it is improbable that we could have got into that extremely strong position so easily as we did, but that in our advance we came upon a small open cable trench leading up to the main trench under the many belts of uncut barbed wire, along which small trench and under the wire we crept in single file into the front trench of the system, and so gradually cleared the way for the rest of the battalion. Why the Germans did not put up a bigger defence is still a mystery to me. This triple line of trenches, that he had so strongly fortified at his leisure so far behind his front line, protected by numerous belts of barbed wire, and with an admirable field of fire that commanded the approach up the slope of Orange Hill for at least a thousand yards was a position that might have been held by a comparatively small number of troops in the face of an army. They must have had the wind up badly. Anyhow, we got into it with remarkably little opposition.

I remember that as we made our way one by one into

the Himalaya Line from that little cable trench, near where we emerged into the main trench there were four badly wounded German soldiers propped up in a row and being attended to by two German "red-cross" men. The latter clamly went on with their work with merely an interested look at us as we pushed in, but the wounded men were in a bad way ; in fact, I saw all four lying there dead a few hours later when I re-visited that part of the captured trenches. When we first came upon them, however, there was one who caused a great deal of mirth to our troops. He was a long lanky fair-haired fellow, and he had been struck by a bullet just under the nose. As he sat propped up against the side of the trench, with his eyes closed and his funny little round German forage cap perched on the extreme crown of his head, his old-fashioned "lug-hook" spectacles had toppled down to the tip of his nose, and in struggling to breathe through the great gash in his nose and palate the poor devil was making a loud snoring noise. Not a very comical sight perhaps, according to civilised ideas, but our men at the time seemed to think it was. And yet those men in their ordinary life at home before the war were probably kind husbands and brothers. War certainly is brutalising. I daresay when nerves were so highly strung it was a case of laugh or cry—and most chose to laugh. Anything was looked upon as a diversion and a relief for the moment.

Another instance of the same kind occurred an hour or so later. My second-in-command, Lieut. McLean, with our two orderlies and his batman worked along to the right towards an artillery track crossing the trenches, beyond which we knew the enemy were still in force. Their snipers had again become very active, and I spotted two of them edging round in the trenches behind us. Having no periscopes with us, I shouted to the others to keep down until we could see what those Boches were up to, but McLean's batman, Rodgers, must needs look over to see for himself. He got one—smack in the middle of the forehead, and he sagged down into a crouching position at the bottom of the trench, the blood trickling down his cheek from the little black hole in his forehead. We of course could see he was stone dead, but as we sat looking at him in consternation for about half a minute, he suddenly heaved a great gusty yawn ! That made us laugh—it seemed so funny to see a dead man yawn !

Grim humour !—as in the case of the man who had his brain-pan carried away by a shell splinter. '' Gosh ! '' remarked one of his comrades, as he surveyed the grisly sight—'' I didna think Geordie has as many brains ! ''

CHAPTER XXXVII

STRONG RESISTANCE WASTES A DAY

WE had captured our main objective, but on our right the 12th Division had not succeeded in penetrating into the German line on account of the thick belts of still intact barbed wire and heavy enemy machine gun fire, the latter being especially hot from the Feuchy Chapel Redoubt, a strong point away to the right astride the Arras-Cambrai road. We were therefore forced to form a defensive flank on the right of our divisional front at a point where the trenches were crossed by a track that had apparently been left open by the Germans for the passage of their artillery and wheeled transport. That flank was repeatedly attacked by the enemy bombers, and at one time they actually attempted to push parties between us and the 12th Division, who had dug themselves in some distance down the slope behind. These attacks we found no great difficulty in beating off, but as we had not sufficient men to take the initiative and clear the enemy from the trenches he still held along to the right, I sent a message to the nearest unit of the 12th Division suggesting that they might make their way gradually by parties into the trenches occupied by us by the same route as we had followed, and so work along and clear the enemy from the trenches on their own divisional front. Nothing was done just then, however, although the commanding officer of the nearest battalion, together with his adjutant, came and took up his quarters in the dugout where I had established my company headquarters, but he seemed rather a helpless sort of fellow. I heard afterwards he was killed that same afternoon. Later on, a company of the Cameron Highlanders from our own 45th Brigade was detailed specially to clear the

enemy from the trenches as far as the Feuchy Chapel
Redoubt, which they did very thoroughly, but it was not
until the next day that the 12th Division got firmly
established in that line. Since the rain in the early morning that day, the
weather had been fairly clear, with spells of sunshine,
but very cold, and towards evening snow began to fall
and kept on intermittently throughout the night. There
was plenty of shelter in those wonderful German trenches,
however, and, except while on our spells of duty out in
the open during the night, we were not too uncomfortable. The dugout in which I had made my company
headquarters was quite a palatial two compartment
affair, with several wire-netting bunks fitted up at the
sides and a deal table in the main compartment. It was
not exactly a dugout, but a solidly built concrete em-
placement reached by three or four steps down from the
trench outside, with embrasures for machine guns commanding a wide view of the approach up the slope in
front. It was in fact a miniature and almost shell-proof
fort. There were others of the same type all along the
Himalaya Line, and the Germans had even covered the
concrete tops of them with green turf, so that they were
almost unnoticeable to an attacking force at any distance.
The one we took over must have been hurriedly evacuated
by its occupants before our arrival, for the electric lights
were still on when we entered, and a half eaten meal lay
on the table. Thrown on the ground, near a sentry's
rifle and bayonet left propped up against the entrance,
we found a cheap paper backed novel folded back where
the reader had just broken off. It was a number of the
" Buffalo Bill Library " in German ; exactly the same
kind of twopenny shocker that used to thrill us in our
boyhood days ! We also found some letters written in
the Danish language, from which we gathered that the
enemy troops we had just displaced belonged to Sleswig.

Next day, a fresh Division, the 37th, passed through
us with the object of capturing Monchy-le-Preux, an

important village on the other side of Orange Hill about two miles beyond the line occupied by us. We ourselves remained inactive all that day, as far as the actual fighting was concerned, but we were otherwise busily employed all the time in consolidating our position in the Himalaya Line, which, although already very strongly fortified as I have said, and magnificently sited from the German's point of view, faced the wrong way for our defence. This consolidation work included the construction of a string of strong points commanding the crest of Orange Hill a few hundred yards in front, in which we were helped by a company of our Divisional Engineers sent up specially for that purpose.

According to our Third Army plan of operations, the 37th Division should have passed through us the day before to the attack on the farther objective, Monchy-le-Preux ; that is, immediately after the Himalaya Line was in our hands and the crest of Orange Hill had been secured by the 15th and 12th Divisions, but as a result of the unforeseen delays in reaching these objectives, especially on the right half of our Corps front, the original time-table was upset.   This was extremely unfortunate as things turned out, for the delay in pressing home the offensive vigorously at that crucial point, while the enemy troops opposed to us were in a state of demoralisation, undoubtedly had an adverse effect on the whole operations.   The respite, short as it was, gave the Germans the opportunity of reorganising in the new positions they had taken up, and of bringing up fresh divisions that made themselves felt immediately.

However, when the 37th Division passed through us that morning in full battle order for the attack, we watched them with the cheerful interest and satisfaction of men who had already accomplished successfully their own particular share of the work, and who now could look on at their leisure while others took up the job. But our part of the show was by no means over, as we later discovered, although at that moment we may have fondly imagined so !

Our commanding officer with the adjutant and myself accompanied one of the support waves of the 37th Division over Orange Hill to watch the progress of the attack, and also to get a good view of Monchy-le-Preux and the valley of the Scarpe beyond. Monchy stood on a knoll of rising ground, and at the time we first saw the village its red roofs appeared almost undamaged by shell fire ; a pretty place, with a large chateau-farm on the northern side surrounded by fruit orchards that were then a mass of pink and white blossom. The last time I saw Monchy-le-Preux, a little over a fortnight afterwards, it was a heap of blackened ruins.

Throughout the day the Boche shelled our positions on the crest of the hill, probably with the intention of preventing reinforcements coming up, and away in front we could see his barrages falling on the troops of the 37th Division, who apparently were meeting with strong opposition to their attacks on Monchy. At one time news came back that the village was captured, but later in the day we heard that the 37th Division had been forced back by determined German counter attacks, and this report seemed to be borne out by the fact that heavy shells from our own long range artillery were still falling on Monchy and the surrounding country.

In the early afternoon a strong cavalry patrol, belonging, I think, to the Essex Yeomanry, rode up through our positions to the top of Orange Hill, where they were immediately met by enemy artillery and machine gun fire that forced them to beat a hurried retreat. The sight of those mounted troops caused us no little surprise, as it was the first time we had ever seen that branch of the army so close to the fighting line.

Later on in the day, while I was in the company dugout writing a situation report, the sergeant-major came in to say that an artillery officer outside wished to speak with me. It was snowing heavily at the time, and as I emerged from the dugout I had another surprise, for there on horseback, towering high above the trench, was a major of the Royal Horse Artillery. He wanted to know whether he could take up a position for his guns in our trench ! This was soon done by running the guns down sloping ways made through the parados wall of the trench, and cutting embrasures for their business ends in the parapet, and within the next hour or so before dusk fell there were several batteries of these R.H.A. 12-pounders blazing away merrily all along Himalaya Trench.

When the snow cleared a little, we saw that a large body of Horse Artillery belonging to the Cavalry Division had come up and were parked on the slope at no great distance behind us, complete with ammunition limbers and all the rest of their transport. Some of the batteries had unlimbered and were already in full action in the open, without any attempt at constructing gun pits or erecting camouflage nets ; not that these precautions would have mattered much, in view of the fact that the whole of their transport and horses were parked in a great mass a short distance down the slope behind them. I saw a good deal of the work of our artillery during the war, but I never saw or heard of anything to equal the quick enterprise of those cavalry artillerymen, who pushed right up to what was really a very precarious line in order that their guns might be in a sufficiently forward position to give effective and badly needed support to the attack of the 37th Division, and to ourselves when we resumed the advance next day. Despite the intensified Boche shelling towards the end of that day, which must have caused them a large number of casualties, in horses as well as men, the artillerymen worked hard at their guns all through the night.

The artillery major whom I mentioned before had made his battery headquarters with us in our company dugout, near the entrance to which one of his guns was posted. He and I happened to be in the dugout when an enemy " whizz-bang " made a direct hit in the trench outside only a yard or two from the gun, instantly killing two of the gunners and badly wounding some other men. We were making our way out to

render help, when the young artillery subaltern in charge
of the section staggered into the dugout and threw
himself on a bunk, his face as white as a sheet, and
vomiting violently. At first we thought he was wounded,
but he was only suffering from shock at the sight outside ; probably it was his first experience of that sort of
thing.

Late that night, or rather about two or three o'clock
in the morning, orders reached us to resume the advance
at 5 a.m. The 37th Division had failed to capture
Monchy-le-Preux, and we, the 15th Division, were to
advance to their assistance, and, if possible, to push on
to a farther objective on a line running roughly north to
the River Scarpe from Boiry-Notre-Dame, a village
about two miles beyond Monchy. To reach the latter
objective meant in all an advance of nearly four miles
from the Himalaya Line, for which task we had to prepare ourselves at that short notice. It must be remembered that we had already suffered heavy casualties,
without any warm food and with hardly any sleep
during the preceding two days, and I am afraid most of
our men were scarcely in a fit condition for the strenuous
work that lay ahead of us. However, their morale was
excellent, and I heard no complaints as we busied ourselves with our preparations in the two or three short
hours that were left to us.

CHAPTER XXXVIII

CAPTURE OF MONCHY-LE-PREUX

AT 5 a.m. on the 11th we resumed our advance in a blinding storm of snow and sleet. The order of attack on this occasion was, ourselves—the 46th Brigade, on the right, and the 45th Brigade on the left, with the 44th remaining in reserve. The morning was dark, and because of the driving snow the visibility was so bad that we could see only a short distance ahead of us, so that it was very difficult to keep touch with the adjoining units, and we had to depend mostly on compass bearings for our direction. In another way the lack of visibility was all in our favour, as it screened the first stage of our advance from view of the German artillery, whose shelling was so haphazard and erratic that we were able to progress for a long distance with comparatively few casualties until the snow began to clear.

My company formed the rear wave of our battalion, which itself was in support to the Brigade, and as we drew near to Monchy, even before the village appeared in view to us, we could hear a great clacking of machine guns and rifle fire arising from that direction, from which commotion we knew that the assault was already being pushed home by the leading waves of our brigade. The snow gradually cleared when we were still some seven or eight hundred yards from Monchy, and as the visibility improved we discovered that almost the whole of the brigade had converged on the village, and that a large part of the 45th Brigade also, which should have advanced with its left flank on the banks of the Scarpe nearly a mile to the left, had veered on to the same objective. To lose direction to that extent, they must have executed almost a complete right wheel in the course of their two mile advance through the snowstorm. Perhaps it was the attraction of the rising ground on which Monchy stood, the tendency always being to proceed direct up the face of a slope, as I have already mentioned, but in any case their wheel brought them up against the blank loop-holed walls on the north side of the village, where they suffered terrible casualties at the hands of the German machine gunners and riflemen.

Part of our battalion joined in the attempt to take the place by direct assault and to clear the enemy from house to house, but they lost heavily in doing so, as did also those battalions of the 37th Division that pushed into the streets of the village, which were swept by fire from the house windows and from every street corner. Although in the defence of a village the odds are all against the attacking force, in all justice to the Germans it must be said that they put up a very stout resistance and held on till the last in Monchy-le-Preux.

Street fighting never pays the attackers, so with my company we skirted the left side of the village and pushed on to a ridge running northeast from Monchy down to the river. There we found ourselves exposed to heavy artillery and machine gun fire, and in the absence of any support on our left, which at the time appeared to be a complete blank between ourselves and the river, we were forced to dig in along a farm track leading out of the village. Our advance was held up, and in fact it was never carried much farther forward in the weeks of fighting that followed, but the position we had secured on the low ridge commanded the approach to Monchy from the enemy's side, and it also prevented the retreat from the village of its defenders. With the 37th Division, which had similarly worked round on the right side, we had almost encircled Monchy, and when a little later we saw enemy shells falling thickly amongst the houses we knew the Germans had given up the place for lost. That made things easier for us, and by sending out parties of men to work *back* through the village we were able to secure the remaining defenders, who on finding themselves shelled by their own artillery apparently lost heart and now surrendered without any further resistance.

The Germans shortly after attempted a counter attack, but it seemed to us a half-hearted affair and was not difficult to stop. For a while after that things quietened down, and as the snow had again commenced to fall there was not much shelling. This quiet spell we made the most of in digging trenches for ourselves and otherwise consolidating our position. It was bitterly cold, and being without greatcoats we put every ounce of energy into the work on those trenches in order to keep ourselves from freezing, though the urgent necessity for the quick construction of some cover was enforced on us every time the snow slackened and the enemy again started to put over shells and bullets in our direction. There is nothing like hostile shelling to stimulate men to the rapid digging of trenches. When enemy shells were landing in their vicinity, the diggers seemed perceptibly to sink into the ground like steam navvies.

CHAPTER XXXIX

CAVALRY IN ACTION

ABOUT this time of the morning, during a lull in the snowstorm, an excited shout was raised that our cavalry were coming up ! Sure enough, away behind us, moving quickly in extended order down the slope of Orange Hill, was line upon line of mounted men covering the whole extent of the hillside as far as we could see. It was a thrilling moment for us infantrymen, who had never dreamt that we should live to see a real cavalry charge, which was evidently what was intended. In their advance the lines of horsemen passed over us rapidly, although from our holes in the ground it was rather a " wormseye " view we got of the splendid spectacle of so many mounted men in action. It may have been a fine sight, but it was a wicked waste of men and horses, for the enemy immediately opened on them a hurricane of every kind of missile he had. If the cavalry advanced over us at the trot or canter, they came back at a gallop, including numbers of dismounted men and riderless horses, and—most fatal mistake of all, they bunched behind Monchy in a big mass, into which the Boche continued to put high-explosive shrapnel, whizz-bangs, and a hail of bullets, until the horsemen dispersed and finally melted away back over the hillside from where they came.

They left a number of dead and wounded men among us, however, but the horses seemed to have suffered most, and for a while after we put bullets into poor brutes that were aimlessly limping about on three legs, or else careering about madly in their agony ; like one I saw that had the whole of its muzzle blown away. With the dead and wounded horses lying about in the snow,

the scene resembled an old-fashioned battle picture.
Why it had been thought fit to send in cavalry at that
juncture, against a strongly reinforced enemy who even
then were holding up our infantry advance, we never
knew. Cavalry may still have their uses in some kinds
of warfare, but for a large force of mounted men to attempt an attack on the enemy positions that day was
sheer madness.

The snow continued on and off throughout the day, and
although there were occasional clear spells in between,
the weather generally was so bad that it practically put
a stop to all operations on both sides for the time being.
Owing to the lack of visibility in the long advance
through the snowstorm that morning, and the subsequent confused fighting in and around Monchy, our
division was inextricably mixed up, men of different units
finding themselves together in the same shell hole without having any idea of the whereabouts of the rest of
their battalion or even company. We endeavoured to
sort ourselves out somewhat, but it was rather a hopeless
task, there being no old trenches or other known places
in the neighbourhood that could be used as fixed rallying
points for the various units. It has to be borne in mind
that we had penetrated far beyond the last trenches of
the old German defence line, and the only cover we had
was in very crude trenches that we had hurriedly made
for ourselves within the past hour or two. As a matter
of fact, most of our Division, and the 37th Division also
on the other side of the village, were scattered over the
countryside in shell holes which they were now linking
up into some sort of defence line, although a very irregular one.

While the snow was falling, and we could move about
more freely without being observed by the Boche machine
gunners and snipers, some of us went out to give what
help we could to the many wounded men lying about
in the open. An extensive orchard belonging to the big
cheateau-farm on the north side of the village was full of
dead and wounded men of our 45th Brigade. As I have

already related, several units of that brigade in their first attack during the morning had swung round against the north side of Monchy, and in the snow beneath the masses of blossom on the fruit trees in that big orchard their dead and wounded were lying in heaps and rows. To add to the horror of it all, since the attack in the early morning in which these men had fallen, the Germans had heavily shelled the orchard and vicinity at the time the cavalry were retiring round that side of the village. As we moved through the orchard in the falling snow, wounded men on every side were shouting and blowing whistles to attract attention, but only too many of them lay like still hummocks of snow. I remember one of these hummocks heaved and cracked open on our approach, as a poor kilted highlander turned over at the sound of our voices. His bare thigh was only a blackened stump, but he complacently and without a murmur accepted the cigarette we lit for him. He, and a great many others of the wounded, must have died that day from loss of blood and exposure. It was a pitiful sight ; the sort of thing that made one rage at the utter futility of it all.

A little later on in the day ; I have no idea now of the exact hour, my watch having stopped, but it must have been about midday, one of my sergeants came to where we were working at the consolidation of a support line and reported that a staff officer had come up. I accompanied the sergeant to where we found two officers waiting in a sheltered part some little distance behind, one of whom I at once perceived to be a general by the gold-laced tabs showing on his collar under the trench coat. The other, a tall dark man, I took to be one of his staff. It was not until afterwards that I learnt that the general officer was Brig.-Gen. Bulkeley-Johnson commanding the 8th Cavalry Brigade, the mounted troops that earlier that morning had made such a disasterous attempt to get through against the enemy. He was a tall fine-looking elderly man, the perfect type of pre-war regular soldier, and I remember he was wearing one of those new-fangled two-piece trench suits over his uniform ; a sort of short waterproof trench coat with separate trousers reaching to below the knee ; under which his gold-laced tabs and cavalry boots could be seen.   His staff officer was attired much the same, and they appeared very spick and span to us mud-plastered infantrymen.   However, the Brigadier wanted to know what the situation was.   I informed him that the enemy in front had been strongly reinforced during the past twenty-four hours, and that instead of our resuming the offensive just then, we were doing our best to consolidate our position to repel another counter attack in force, which was expected at any time.   Also that the enemy were especially concentrating around the village of Pelves down on our half-left front by the river.   The Brigadier thought he would like to see something of the enemy dispositions for himself, and I told him it could be done, but that to reach a point of vantage on the low ridge in front, the snow having cleared just then, the greatest caution was required, and that if the German snipers spotted us it would be necessary to dodge them by sprinting diagonally from shell hole to shell hole as we did.   Nevertheless, the General insisted on going on against my advice, and perhaps being rather old for that sort of active dodging, or, as it seemed to me at the time, too dignified to get well down at the sound of a bullet, he would persist in walking straight on.   That of course was deadly, as I well knew.   I led the little procession, and sure enough as soon as we reached the ridge a fusilade of bullets hummed around our ears.   We had not got far when one skimmed past me and struck the General full on the cheekbone.   I shall never forget his piercing shriek as he tumbled down and rolled over on the ground. As for the staff officer and myself, we dived for the nearest shell hole, where we found two signallers of the Royal Scots of the 45th Brigade, whom I got to crawl out with me and bring in the General.   We had to be very careful, as all the German riflemen seemed by then to be concentrating their attention on our locality, but by working backwards on our bellies we succeeded in dragging the General to the shell hole. However, he died as we were getting him there. I did not see the staff officer after that, so presumably he managed to make his own way back.

After I returned to my company and the snow had come on again, I went out with a party and brought back the General's body to our support line, where it was laid on the parados of the trench we had constructed. Things were quiet for a while after that, and as I sat there idly contemplating the body and watching the snow flakes settling gently on the blue upturned dead face with its grizzled moustache, I could not help reflecting that there lay a well known professional soldier, whose whole life had been devoted to the study of war, and yet he was killed the first time he got within rifle range of a really formidable enemy, while we amateur soldiers who had known nothing about soldiering only a year or two before, still kept on surviving and coping with the most highly trained troops the Germans could put in the field against us.

CHAPTER XL

RELIEVED

THE expected counter attack did not materialise, or at least did not reach our part of the line, and except for intermittent bombardments by the enemy artillery, the rest of the day passed without any further incident worthy of mention. Whenever the snow ceased for any length of time and there was some visibility, German aeroplanes hovered overhead reconnoitring the line taken up by our troops, about the exact position of which the enemy appeared to be in some doubt at the time. These hostile aircraft met with very little opposition from our own airmen as far as we saw, and some of them flew so low over us that we were able to open fire on them from the ground with rifles and lewis guns. We knew very well that enemy air reconnaissances, if allowed to be carried out unmolested, were invariably followed by intensive and more accurate shelling by the German artillery.

The following night passed quietly, but it again was a sleepless one for us because of the intense cold, even had it been possible to find a comfortable resting place at the bottom of the muddy shell holes and rough trenches we occupied. And yet some men dozed off from sheer exhaustion while on their feet, leaning against the cold wet side of the trench or hole. In the miserable weather that had been the rule during the three days since we left the cellars in Arras, they had had no warm food, and the emergency rations of hard biscuits and bully beef with which we had started were now all finished. There is no doubt that at this stage our men were physically played out and quite unfit to take part in any further operations just then.

Early next morning, the 12th, which opened fine and sunny, though still very cold, we were relieved by a battalion of the Yorks. and Lancs. of the 17th Division, who came up across the open in small detached parties to take over the line from us. In the same manner we made our way back to a rendezvous in the Railway Triangle near the original German front line, where the battalion assembled, and that afternoon we moved farther back to billets in Arras.

We found that changes had taken place in the city in the few days since the opening of the offensive. Whereas the movement of large bodies of men was forbidden before in the daytime, the streets now presented a busy scene ; being packed with bodies of troops and transport, and especially with long lines of artillery moving up to new positions. The street barricades had all been removed, and the maze of entanglements were cleared from the centre of the Grand Place, which now no longer justified its old name of " Barbed-Wire Square." But what most impressed us was the sight of the ruined railway station and the adjoining traffic yard, from which, after lying derelict for over two years under a continuous enemy bombardment, the litter of wrecked rolling stock had been entirely cleared, and the railway put in working order to a point well beyond the old German front line. Trains laden with repair material were already running to near Feuchy village, the scene of some of the hardest fighting only three days before. I heard that this quick work was mostly accomplished by a Canadian Railway unit.

But although the enemy had been driven back from Arras to beyond ordinary field gun bombardment distance, the city was still well within the reach of his long range artillery, and he did not let us forget it. We saw evidence of that as we were entering by one of the streets on the eastern side, where an hour or two before a press of artillery and other horse transport had been caught by a whole salvo of heavy shells. Some of the debris of the horses was still scattered around and festooned on the trees along the street. The enemy aircraft were also busy over the city, and while we were there an air bomb penetrated through the street pavement into a cellar occupied by men of the 10/11th H.L.I. of our brigade, causing a large number of casualties. Judging by the frequency and apparent immunity with which the enemy airmen flew over, I think the Germans must have had the upper hand in that branch of the fighting just then, but in all fairness to our Flying Corps it must be said that a large congested city such as Arras, still so near the fighting line, must have presented an easy mark to the enemy air bombers, who could not always be intercepted, especially after dark.

We spent two days in Arras resting and cleaning up, although while there we were still in support, and therefore alert in case of an emergency at the fighting front. The big offensive had died down, however, and although a good deal of stiff fighting still continued, as we heard, it was more for the purpose of straightening our line and consolidating the positions already won than with the object of pressing forward the advance on a large scale. Within little over a week we were in it again up to the eyebrows, but just then, for the time being at any rate, we felt rather satisfied with what we had done, and in fact an Army Order was published complimenting the 15th Scottish Division on their achievements in that first phase of the Arras battle. In three days we had broken into the German lines to a depth of just over four miles ; through the front trench system he had occupied and strengthened for more than two years, through his strong reserve line—the formidable Himalaya system, and far beyond that we had taken from him the village of Monchy-le-Preux, a position dominating the farther valley of the River Scarpe. In this advance I believe more than forty guns were captured by the Division, beside a large number of prisoners. Our own losses in these three days were heavy of course, the casualties in my company (" A " Company) totalling to a man exactly half the number we took into the attack, but our

" C " Company, and I believe some other units of the Division, lost even more heavily.

After two days in billets in Arras we were moved back to reserve in the neighbourhood of Duisans, and I remember that as we marched out of the city, our Divisional Commander, Maj.-Gen. McCracken, with his staff, had taken up a position just outside the Porte Baudimont to review us as we passed. We were pleased at that, though I am afraid our numbers were so few that as a battalion we could not have created much of an impression.

The march back was not a long one, only some eight or nine kilometers, but even after the two days' rest in the cellars in Arras it was fatiguing for a lot of the men, who had not altogether recovered as yet from the trying time they had so recently gone through, so we went slowly. However, their morale was wonderfully good, all things considered. After a really hard time in the line, it was always fine to see how quickly most of them recovered their usual cheerful spirits immediately we got back to support or reserve and they had had a hot meal or two, and how they seemed to forget entirely that such a thing as a war was still going on only a few kilometers away, with the never remote chance of our being plunged again into the muck of it at a few hours' notice. Of course there were always the despondent and embittered ones, and also some men of advanced political ideas who did their best in their own way to create trouble among the rest, but they were few. On the other hand we had our full share of the bright and irresponsible spirits ; at least one was to be found in every platoon ; those " comics " whose good humour and lively wit provided the leaven that kept the majority cheerful even under the most trying conditions. As, for instance, towards the end of a fatiguing march, when many of the men were glum, and some of them perhaps approaching the last stage of exhaustion. It was then that a song started by one of those natural optimists, at first taken up rather half-heartedly, would develop into a real enthusiastic chorus joined in by all, and the tired and drooping ones would again square their shoulders and forget their woes for the time being.

These marching songs were usually parodies of old popular songs at home. I remember one that was sung to the tune of a long-forgotten music hall song that was popular in my early youth—and that is a long time ago. The original song was entitled " She only answered Ting-a-ling-a-ling," but the version as sung by our troops on the march went :—

"The bells of hell go ting-a-ling-a-ling
"For you as well as me,
"Oh, Death, where is thy sting-a-ling-a-ling,
"Oh, Grave, thy victoree !

There were many others, such as the " Three Little Maids from Khandahar," that I dare not repeat—they were scarcely parlour songs, although very popular with the troops at that time.

Besides many marching songs of their own, the troops when in billets had a lot of catch-words and phrases that would be difficult to explain now. One of them, I remember, was that a man would suddenly shout at the pitch of his voice " Some say ' Good old Sergeant ' ! " The stereotyped response to that was bellowed in chorus " But WE say...........! "—with great emphasis on the " we." Any man who served in the 15th Division or any other Scottish unit will be able to fill in the rest of that battle cry for himself ! These japes were always in good humour, however, though needless to say they were not indulged in when " good old sergeant " was within earshot. Nevertheless, when passing at night along the dark roads in the vicinity of the men's billets, we could recognise the shout ; all the N.C.O.'s and so many of our officers having themselves gone through it in the ranks.

CHAPTER XLI

In Reserve

WE remained some days in reserve at the small village of Agnez-lez-Duisans resting and refitting, and while there we received several drafts of reinforcements from the Base, whose numbers, however, fell short of our recent losses. Apart from a percentage of returned wounded men, the fresh drafts that were joining us about that time were rather poor material, being composed to a great extent of conscripts and previously rejected men who were now being called up for the army. Among the conscripts were some peculiar characters, and I remember that in the batch allotted to my own company were two or three Polish miners from the Lanarkshire coalfields who could scarcely speak English ! Those strange recruits to the Highland Light Infantry all bore good Scotch names, which no doubt they had adopted because their own names were almost unpronouncable to us. However, in the short course of intensive training we were able to put these new recruits through before returning to the front line, they mostly proved themselves very willing, despite flat feet and other infirmities. Fortunately, we still continued to receive a certain number of old regular soldiers of the original 1st and 2nd Battalions of the H.L.I., who helped to maintain a stiff backbone in our battalion.

Orders for the move back to the front reached us on the 17th or 18th, and that same day I was sent on ahead of the battalion to Arras on some special duty, I forget what, accompanied by 2/Lieut. McQueen of "C" Company, who had been detailed to act as forward billeting officer. We set out on foot, but on reaching the main road we obtained a lift in a motor ambulance that took us all the way to Arras. I remember that as we passed into the city through the Porte Baudimont in that ambulance, McQueen jokingly wondered whether we would be brought back that way in one of these vehicles, or whether we would ever come back at all. He did not.

The battalion arrived next day and took up quarters in the old familiar cellars, although the men were not now confined underground during the daytime, as had been the rule up till some ten days before, when the German front line ran so close to the city. In fact, many of the houses, or at least their lower stories, were now being utilised as open billets for troops, the risk from shellfire above ground I daresay being considered no greater than the danger of sickness breaking out amongst the men in the stuffy subterranean cellars. The enemy long-range artillery were still putting over heavy shells, however, and one of these on the first night went right through the front of the house occupied by our Battalion Headquarters, but without causing any casualties.

These two or three days spent in Arras prior to the opening of the second phase of the big offensive were employed in completing the equipment of our men with extra ammunition and bombs, picks and shovels, stokes-mortar shells (for clearing enemy dugouts), and all the rest of the paraphernalia carried nowadays by infantry going into a big attack. As I have already mentioned, many of the new men who had just joined us were of poor physique or over age, and when fully loaded in battle order they were often incapable of bearing the burden for any distance or length of time over rough ground. The result was that when the material carried by them was really needed, it was frequently found to have been discarded on the way by those lame ducks!

The front of the 15th Division in the impending resumption of the attack was to be astride the Arras/ Cambrai road, some distance to the south of the ground covered by us in our recent advance, and as it was new to us, a reconnaissance of the front to be taken over was made one day by the commanding officer with the adjutant and company commanders. Our small party rode out of Arras through the old German trenches and along the Arras/Cambrai road to a point about fifteen hundred yards west of the Himalaya Line, where we left our horses in charge of the mounted orderlies in a hollow in which we thought they would be screened from enemy shellfire. From there we proceeded on foot across the Himalaya Trenches to the rise beyond, from where we obtained a good view through our glasses of the ground held by the enemy and of the village of Guemappe, which was to be one of our objectives. So far we had been unmolested, though German aeroplanes were hovering overhead, but on our return to the hollow where the horses were picketed we found enemy shells landing all around the vicinity. The poor brutes were frantic with fright, and although fortunately none of them was injured, they were almost unmanageable for the time being, and they gave us rather an exciting time for the first part of the ride back to Arras. On that excursion I saw that the slope of Orange Hill was still littered with the dead horses left by our cavalry nine or ten days before, though all the saddlery and equipment had been removed. Dead horses, with their big grinning teeth, are always an ugly sight, and they certainly give .a tang to the air !

On the afternoon of the 22nd we moved forward to front line reserve, where we took up a position in the old German support trenches in the neighbourhood of the Bois-des-Boeufs, between the Cambrai and Wancourt roads. These trenches were over a mile to the south of that part of the line we ourselves had captured in the last attack, but like all the other enemy trenches we had seen on the Arras front, we found them very strongly constructed ; with deep and spacious dugouts that ran like tunnels all along the line, and which must have been capable of providing comparative safe accommodation for a large number of troops, even under the heaviest bombardments. Having little to do that evening and the following morning, being still so far behind the actual fighting line that only a few sentries were necessary, we had ample leisure to make a thorough inspection of the trenches and dugouts so recently occupied by the enemy, a recreation that always greatly interested us.

In those dugouts we used to find all sorts of kit left by the Germans, sometimes even officers' swords, but always plenty of bayonets with their tri-coloured tassels ; the three colours of the tassel denoting the battalion, company and platoon a man belonged to. The bayonets were of various sizes and shapes, some short and stubby like the bayonet formerly used by our army with the old martini-henri rifle ; others long and very similar to our own present day bayonet, and occasionally we came across small bayonets that looked like gully-knives with clips for fixing on a rifle. I imagine those latter were not a regulation German army issue, however, but merely " sports," like the trench-daggers and suchlike fancy blood-thirsty gadgets that used to be for sale in the Sports Department of Gamages and other outfitters in the early days of the war. These things did not count for much, because they were not often used ; at least, not that I ever saw. Sometimes we found on dead Germans, or hidden away in their dugouts, long bayonets with a terrible saw-edge on the back. God help the live German we caught carrying one of those barbarous weapons.

CHAPTER XLII

At it Again—Capture of Guemappe

The second Arras battle opened at about 5 a.m. on the 23rd of April. On this occasion, as I said before, our divisional front was a mile or two south of the scene of our previous attack, and the main objectives allotted to us were the village of Guemappe and a strong enemy position known as Cavalry Farm, with a further possible objective on a line running roughly along the ridge between St. Rohart Factory and the Bois-du-Vert, that is, about two miles beyond the foremost positions then held by the enemy. On our right, on the other side of a small stream named the Cojeul, was the 50th Division, and on the left of the attacking line, the 29th Division, while the 3rd Division was in Corps reserve around Arras. In our own Division the attack was led off by the 44th and 45th Brigades, with ourselves, the 46th, in support as before, but once again we found that being in support usually ends up in the thickest part of the fighting.

Throughout the forenoon, after the attack had commenced, we (the 46th Brigade) remained inactive in the old German support trenches, kicking our heels and listening to the sounds of battle away in the distance ahead of us, but towards mid-day we received orders to move forward to the Himalaya Line. There it was soon apparent that things were not going too well with the 44th and 45th Brigades, and although it seemed that during the forenoon they had taken Guemappe and pushed their advance some distance beyond, the Germans were counter attacking heavily, and had not only recaptured the village, but recovered most of the ground lost by them earlier in the day. On our flanks, the 50th and 29th Divisions also had failed to make much permanent headway, and at one time in the afternoon, when the enemy were again about to launch a strong counter attack, matters were so serious that an order came through that, in the event of our foremost brigades being forced farther back, the Himalaya Line was to be held at all costs. The staff must have taken rather a gloomy view of the situation just then.

From German prisoners coming back through us at that time we learnt that among the troops opposed to us were our old friends the 3rd Bavarian Division. They apparently knew it too, for in an '' Order of the Day '' found on one of these prisoners, it was specially mentioned that the 3rd Bavarian Division were once again up against the 15th Scottish Division, '' which they had already met and *defeated* at the Battle of Loos and at Martinpuich on the Somme ! '' We always considered the Bavarians the toughest brand of Germans we ever met. There was no doubt about it ; they were good soldiers.

Late in the afternoon we were ordered to advance through the 44th and 45th Brigades and take Guemappe and Cavalry Farm, together with the ridge beyond that had formed the first objective that morning, and about 5 o'clock we went over to the attack. The Brigade advanced as usual in widely extended order, but we had not progressed far before the Boche, who evidently was prepared for this move on our part, put down an artillery barrage on us. His shelling was scrappy at first, but as we went on it became so intensified that we were brought to a halt and forced to take cover in the shell holes around us, where we lay doggo until the barrage died down.

At this indecisive stage, while I was working from shell hole to shell hole trying to collect my company, which had become somewhat mixed up with the others, as always happened on these occasions, I met Capt. Hannah of '' D '' Company, and together we went forward to ascertain the situation in front. Even the movement of us two men, although we of course kept widely separated and moved quickly, attracted the notice of some of the enemy gunners, who must have had alert observers on the rising ground before us, but it was their snipers who worried us most in that quick sprint across the open. We found that on the right most of the 44th Brigade were back almost to their original line along a farm road shown on our maps as Spear Lane, although isolated parties were still holding out in shell holes a few hundred yards in front and in a German trench to the northwest of Guemappe. On the left, more progress seemed to have been made by the 45th Brigade, but there also the advance had been held up at no great distance. Hannah and I pushed on our reconnaissance to beyond the German trench just mentioned, and although it was apparent that the enemy was very much in strength on the higher ground on both our flanks in front of the 50th and 29th Divisions, and that he still strongly held at least the northern outskirts of Guemappe, it did not seem that there was a great deal of opposition up the shallow valley directly ahead of us. From what we saw for ourselves, and also what we learnt from some isolated men of the 44th Brigade whom we found in an advanced shell hole, it appeared that the leading waves of the last enemy counter attack were dispersed in shell holes, much the same as we were ourselves. This seemed our opportunity, and accordingly, while Hannah remained in that advanced shell hole to await his company, I sprinted back to report on the situation to the other company commanders, and for that matter to the whole of the right half of our brigade ; for we were all mixed up in shell holes scattered all over that part of the landscape where our advance had been held up.

On the return journey, a matter of nearly a thousand yards, I made my way as rapidly as I could across the open, but the German snipers spotted me, and several times in the course of that sprint, on hearing the " whisp " of bullets about my ears, I had to make hurried dives into the nearest shell hole to escape their attentions. One of these holes, I remember, happened to contain three dead Germans, who only too obviously had lain there for several days, and I slid right on top of them before I had time to notice their presence. In the ordinary way I would have remained doggo in that shell hole until the enemy riflemen lost interest in my whereabouts, but the stench was too utterly horrible to be borne. I decided quickly that, snipers or no snipers, I would rather be cleanly shot than asphyxiated, so I took the " death in the fresh air " alternative and sprinted to another hole, from which I eventually managed to work my way back unharmed, though still suffering from nausea.

The German snipers with their telescopic rifle-sights were deadly, and it was sheer suicide to walk in a straight line across the open within their view. The only way it could be done without discomfort was to sprint diagonally from shell hole to shell hole, without giving any indication of the next direction to be taken, and without allowing them time to get their telescopic sights well laid on. The man who heard bullets whisp by him and disdained to take quick cover was a fool. Bullets in flight can only be heard when passing very close, therefore the very fact that they are heard at all should in itself indicate that the hearer is the intended mark. Although the bullets that are heard have of course missed, the next one might not.

On regaining my company, the advance was resumed by the whole battalion. As soon as we got well going, the enemy barrage recommenced, but it was not so intense as before, and we pressed on through the 44th and 45th Brigades ; skirting the northern side of Guemappe, but leaving the village itself severely alone. We knew only too well from our recent experience in Monchy-le-Preux that village street fighting is an unpaying proposition for attacking troops, and that the best way to deal with these obstacles is to skirt and outflank them, if it can be done. As at Monchy, the blackened ruins of which we could then see on the rising ground away to the north, the enemy abandoned Guemappe when he saw that we had advanced beyond it.

The enemy artillery barrage, for unknown reasons, was not too intense at this stage of our advance, perhaps because his guns were in process of being removed further back, but his machine-gun and rifle fire was very hot, and we were particularly annoyed by two low-flying German aeroplanes that followed and machine-gunned us ; " zooming " down on us, then swooping up again to repeat the manœuvre from the rear. One of these aeroplanes was brought down by rifle fire from the ground, I think by some men of the 44th Brigade in the shell holes over which we were passing, and I remember it landed with a terrific crash about fifty yards from where I was, its engine roaring like a million beehives for a few seconds before it burst into flames and was silent. It had " zoomed " down a little too far that time !

With less opposition than we expected, as the 50th and 29th Divisions also were now advancing on our flanks, we pressed on past the northern outskirts of Guemappe, but on approaching to within four or five hundred yards of Cavalry Farm our advance was again held up by hot machine gun and rifle fire from that enemy stronghold, as well as from the slopes of the ridges on our right and left. We were supposed to be in support to the 10th Scottish Rifles of our brigade, but since the onset of the advance the two battalions had become mixed up, and together we were compelled to dig ourselves in along a line within about three hundred yards of Cavalry Farm, our main body being in a roughly made German trench some little distance behind.

On the right, some of the Scottish Rifles with our " D " Company (Capt. Hannah) had pushed on and taken up a line about a hundred yards or so beyond the farm, and on the left we could see that the 10/11th H.L.I. had progressed well up the slope of the ridge that formed the line of our first objective, but the stiff opposition we encountered at Cavalry Farm held up the advance on

our own part of the front. It was getting late in the
evening, and although the buildings seemed to be a nest
of German machine gunners determined to hold on at all
costs, I think Cavalry Farm might have been taken just
then, but that our own heavy artillery were putting shells
into it and all around its neighbourhood, and at intervals
during the night and even the next day they continued
to bombard the place. If they had ceased this shelling
of the Farm when we got to within real attacking
distance, we might have dealt with it, but they made it a
shell trap not only for the defenders, who had the cover
of their dugouts, but also for any attacking force that
approached too near. As a matter of fact, during the
night when things were quieter for the time being, I
and one of my sergeants (Sgt. Ramage) went out on
patrol, and by creeping up a ditch that ran along the
bottom of the Cambrai road embankment, near which
stood Cavalry Farm, we passed that enemy stronghold
in the darkness almost without knowing it. Em-
boldened by the quietness of the place just then, we
made a closer inspection of that side of the position on
our way back, and on the western outskirts of the Farm
we saw a number of Germans crouching along the side of
a shallow sunken path. Unless they were all dead or
asleep they must have seen and heard us, for we passed
within only a few yards of them, but perhaps in the pitch
darkness they thought we were two of their own men
going out on patrol. It would scarcely occur to them
that two of the enemy, for whom they were watching
so intently in front, would pass through them from
behind. Fortunately, we kept our heads and did not get
panicky, but needless to say it was with great relief
that the sergeant and I reached the friendly cover of our
roadside ditch. Cavalry Farm was not finally captured
until two days later, and then only after several bombardments by our heavy artillery and a good deal of stiff
fighting. Our friends the Bavarians held out stoutly in
that position till the last.

CHAPTER XLIII

A CHECK AT CAVALRY FARM

NEXT morning, things remained somewhat stagnant in our section of the line in front of Cavalry Farm, which was still being intermittently, and, as we thought, rather futilely shelled by our heavy artillery, but on the slope of the ridge on the other side of the Cambrai road to the left we could see that our 10/11th H.L.I. and the 7/8th K.O.S.B.'s, who had come up to support them, were having a busy time in the face of a succession of determined German counter attacks. These enemy attacks were in every case preluded by hurricane artillery barrages all along the line, including our position in front of the Farm, but if any infantry counter attacks were intended in our own particular direction at that time they did not amount to much. On the slope to our left, however, the 10/11th H.L.I. were giving way, and we could see them coming back down the hillside, though without panic, and still in the same good extended order in which they had advanced. At this stage, the 50th and 29th Divisions on our flanks were also forced back some distance, which left us exposed to enemy machine gun and rifle fire from the higher ground on both sides.

Some time in the afternoon we had orders to resume the attack, and this time the 10th Scottish Rifles, to whom we were originally intended to be in support before we became mingled with them, were allotted Cavalry Farm as their special objective, while we, the 12th H.L.I., were to execute a diagonal movement to the left across the Cambrai road, and advance up the slope covered by our sister battalion the evening before and recently evacuated by them.

This fresh attack, which I think was started sometime

about 4 o'clock in the afternoon, did not open well for
us, because the enemy just at that time was evidently
intending something of the same thing on his own account, and a few minutes before we left our cover for the
advance, he laid down a murderous barrage on us. I
remember that as we were clambering out to the open
ground, one of my company orderlies had his head blown
away, and I think we suffered a lot of casualties in those
unfortunate few minutes ; just because our " going-
over " happened to coincide with the artillery preparation by the enemy for an attack of his own.

However, in the confusion of that moment we sorted
ourselves out as best we could from the Scottish Rifles,
and deploying to our left across the Cambrai road
according to plan, we skirted Cavalry Farm and pushed
on through the smoke and din of the bursting shells
right to the crest of the ridge, an advance of nearly a
thousand yards. There the reception we met with
from the enemy machine gunners and riflemen was so
fierce that we could proceed no further, and we were
forced to take cover as quickly as we could in shell holes
and any other shelter we could find. Our position was a
precarious one, as we were right in amongst the Germans,
who, although they did not appear to have any regular
trench line on the hill top, being in shell holes that they
had had time to deepen and otherwise fortify, were in
considerable strength, with an unusually large number
of machine guns. Moreover, the Scottish Rifles had
failed to take Cavalry Farm, so that we were now en-
filaded by fire from that position in our right rear. On
our left, the 7/8th K.O.S.B.'s, who were attacking on that
side, had not made so much progress as ourselves, thus
leaving a wide gap between us and the 29th Division on
our left flank, which was therefore in danger of being
turned by the enemy at any moment.

The situation was precarious and dangerous for us,
as I have said, as the slightest movement in the open
immediately attracted a fusilade of bullets from the
enemy around us, but it was equally dangerous for him

to show himself just then, although the German troops holding the ridge were numerically much stronger than ourselves, and far better provided with machine guns. It was about that time that three officers of " C " Company, Lieut. Chislett and 2/Lieuts. McQueen and Watson, were shot dead in quick succession while trying to reach a shell hole close to where I had dug myself in. Why they wanted to get to that particular hole I never knew. They came over singly, running and crouching low, and knowing the danger I yelled on them to keep down, but either they did not hear or disregarded the warning, and I saw them topple forward one after the other all within the space of about five minutes.

This state of checkmate, in which little or no open movement could be made on the crest of the ridge by either side, continued for the few remaining hours of daylight, but when darkness fell we endeavoured to sort ourselves out from the enemy, in the course of which there was a good deal of bombing and close fighting throughout the night. In this work, and in the construction of something like a trench line, with a communication trench running to the rear, we were greatly assisted by our Pioneer Battalion, the 9th Gordons, who came up specially for that purpose in the evening and returned before dawn. On the left also, some of the 7/8th K.O.S.B.'s moved forward in the night and formed a line of strong points linking up the gap between us and the 29th Division, whose right flank battalion we discovered were entrenched some two or three hundred yards half-left behind us. This consolidation work was not allowed to proceed uninterrupted by the Boche, and more than once that night he put down an intense artillery barrage, no doubt with the intention of preventing reinforcements coming up to us ; we ourselves being so close up against his own foremost troops that the shelling passed harmlessly over our heads. It passed so close, however, that the crash of the high-explosive shrapnel bursting only a few yards above us was terrific, though the effect of these shells would only be felt some distance down the slope behind us.

During the night some reinforcements nevertheless managed to reach us from Battalion H.Q., including our reserve lewis-gun teams. One of these lewis-gunners belonging to my own company, I remember, was a man named Clancy (another of our remaining bantams) ; a slovenly little tough, whose unclean appearance had always been an eye-sore to me on parade. In the darkness, Clancy passed through us and found himself right amongst the Germans, where he took refuge in a shell hole, which, fortunately for him, happened to be unoccupied. There he lay undiscovered for the rest of that night and the whole of the following day, but getting impatient towards evening before it was properly dark, he decided to make a sprint for it back to our lines. On his way he was fired at not only by the enemy, but also by some of our own men, who in the gathering dusk mistook him for a German, yet by some wonderful chance he succeeded in reaching us unharmed—and still carrying the two heavy buckets of lewis-gun ammunition he had brought up with him the night before ! We badly needed that ammunition, which he could not have been blamed for discarding to lighten himself in his dangerous sprint, but he stuck to it throughout. Some time afterwards, I asked Clancy how he had liked his day among the enemy. His reply was a scowl and —" It would tak' mair than they Germans tae put the wind up me ! "

Despite the fact that, with Cavalry Farm and its energetic defenders still holding out and enfilading us from the half-right rear, and with the 29th Division entrenched some distance behind on the left, we were in a very exposed salient on the ridge, we clung on to every foot of the ground we had gained, and by morning we had consolidated our position into a more or less connected line. The next day passed quietly enough, but as no ration parties were able to get up to us, and we had long since exhausted the emergency rations and water we carried with us at the commencement of the attack, not to speak of the lack of sleep during the preceding two nights, we were once again beginning to feel played out physically and mentally. Fortunately the weather continued fine all the time, and we did not suffer from exposure to anything like the same extent as in those terrible few days around Monchy a fortnight previously. Neither did we starve altogether, for many of our men proved themselves expert foragers, and by crawling to adjacent shell holes they managed to gather a fair quantity of emergency rations from dead Germans ; a kind of compressed sausage meat in hermetically sealed tins, which we rather liked, although it was not new to many of us who had in the same way on previous occasions '' dined with the enemy '' so to speak. No rations nor water were to be found on our own dead, who of course had been as hungry as the rest of us when they met their end there.

The following night we were relieved by a unit of the 45th Brigade and moved back to reserve, where we took up a position along a road running out of the ruined hamlet of Marliere, near Wancourt, that is, on approximately the original front line held by our Division before the attack. Although a good two thousand yards or more behind the new fighting line, we found it a very '' shelly '' neighbourhood, perhaps because the Boche imagined it might be a concentrating point for troops brought up for a fresh attack, which certainly was not the case just then.

At any rate, he shelled us intermittently all the time we were there, and we soon discovered that to show much movement, and especially to show the smoke of a fire, immediately drew his artillery fire afresh. On our first morning there, a supply of rations having just come up, one of our batmen, unknown to us, but foolishly, though perhaps meaning well, made a small fire on the bank of the road just above where we were sitting at the time, and while he was bending over his cooking, a '' whizz-bang '' scattered him and our breakfast, fire and all. That was only a chance hit of course, but it indicated that we were still under direct observation of the enemy, who must have had a large and very efficient concentration of artillery against us at this stage of the operations, when he could afford to give so much attention to our back areas at the same time as he was so heavily barraging our front line and immediate supports.

Nevertheless, we were able to get some much needed rest while we remained in reserve along that road near Marliere, despite the shelling and the occasional necessity for us to " stand-to " whenever a hubbub of fireworks away in front indicated a fresh outbreak of activity in that direction, as happened once or twice. We took turns at relieving one another, and I remember I slept for about six hours on end as sound as a log in a little dugout which we made the *combined* headquarters of " A " and " C " Companies. The dugout was only a few feet square, a mere cubby-hole of no depth excavated in the bank of the road, and having been made by the Germans it was of course on the wrong side of the road and now fully exposed to their shell fire, but it was big enough to accommodate us. Of the two companies, only three officers were left, 2/Lieut. Donnelly and myself of "A" Company, and 2/Lieut. Main of " C " Company.

CHAPTER XLIV

A WELCOME REST

ON the following day, the 27th, the 56th Division relieved us, and after what seemed a long and weary trek over the scarred battlefield back to Arras; astonishingly long to us at the time because the distance we covered gave some indication of the extent of the ground that had been captured in the past fortnight, we went into billets in Arras for the night. On arrival in the city, after seeing the company settled down and food served out to the men, Donnelly and I, while on the way to our own billet, looked in at Battalion Headquarters. Some of the people there appeared surprised to see me, having heard that I had been killed. It seemed that the battalion orderly who brought back that report from the front line said that, while lying in a shell hole waiting for dusk, he had heard several rifle shots and seen me drop suddenly. His report of what he saw no doubt was correct enough, because to get down slick at the crack of an enemy rifle was just the first thing I would do. I was always a believer in the old adage that says '' A live donkey is better than a dead lion,'' which, although not very heroic, perhaps helped me to keep on surviving.

Next day we were moved back to hutments near Duissans, where we remained resting and refitting for a day or two before going farther back to Corps reserve. It was at Duissans that I was surprised and delighted to learn I had been granted ten days' leave ; my first home leave since I joined the 15th Division in France. Needless to say, I lost no time in stuffing a few necessities into my pack and hopping on to a G.S. wagon that took me to St. Pol and the railway. Two days later I was in civilian clothes (which seemed very slack on me), and listening to what people at home were saying about the recent operations at Arras. On one occasion in a restaurant smokeroom, I remember meeting an acquaintance who told me that on my entering the smokeroom the friends he was sitting with had expressed surprise that a big fellow like me was not in the army! I wondered myself why many of the men I saw there were not.

On my return from that all too short leave I found the battalion billetted at Fosseux, a small village some distance back from Arras, in our Corps reserve area. In my absence a large number of new officers and men had joined us, so that half the battalion now appeared strangers to me. I also discovered to my regret that " A " Company, which I had commanded for so long, had been taken over by a newly arrived captain, and that I was now attached to Battalion Headquarters; in what capacity I never quite knew, as there was already a Second-in-Command and also a spare major on our strength. From then on for the few weeks that I remained with the battalion I seemed to be a sort of supernumerary company commander attached to Battalion H.Q., sometimes acting in command of one company, then another, as occasion required. On the other hand, on my arrival back from leave I was cheered somewhat to hear that I had been recommended for a decoration, which, however, never materialised.

For the next week or two, we spent a pleasant and not too strenuous time at Fosseux and other villages in that area, although our Division was still in Corps reserve and in the expectation of being sent into the line again at any moment. Nothing happened, however, the big operations in front of Arras having apparently died down, and towards the end of May the whole Division, artillery and all, was withdrawn a long way back to Army reserve. The march was made by easy stages spread over two or three days, and as the weather was splendid all the time the troops were in fine fettle and full of spirits.

It was at one of the halts on that march that my company fell out close to an army carrier-pigeon loft belonging to the Corps Signallers. These pigeon lofts were mobile affairs built on a motor chassis, and they were always objects of great interest to our men, many of whom were keen pigeon fanciers. As these enthusiasts sat by the roadside regarding the loft and holding an expert discussion on carrier pigeons, one wag was heard to express the opinion that better results might be obtained if the pigeons were crossed with cockatoos, so that they could be trained to deliver messages verbally ! The suggestion is offered to the War Office for what it is worth.

While on this subject, I once heard a story of a Corps Commander who had occasion to feel somewhat disappointed in the carrier pigeon branch of his signal service. An offensive was in progress at the front line, but although signallers with carrier pigeons had been sent forward with the infantry, no news had yet come through as to how the attack was faring. Therefore, when it was reported that a pigeon was approaching from the battle front, the general with the senior officers of his staff hurried out and eagerly gathered around the loft while the sergeant signaller secured the pigeon and detached the message from its leg. All that was written on the paper was " I am fed up with this bloody bird ! " It was said that the signallers used to eat the pigeons when no fresh rations were forthcoming.

The destination of our battalion was Buire-au-Bois, a village four or five kilometers north of the town of Auxi-le-Chateau, fully fifty kilometers west of Arras and far beyond the sounds of war. Buire-au-Bois (which of course our Jocks rendered as " Beery Boys ") is a pretty little place situated in a deep valley in the midst of a hilly and wooded countryside, and I always look back on the three weeks we spent there as the pleasantest time I ever knew in France. I was quartered in the house of the village cure, a dear old man who did everything he possibly could to make me comfortable. It was luxurious to have a neat bedroom with a clean bed to sleep in once again.

AND ALL FOR WHAT?

There is nothing of much interest to record during this three weeks stay in Army Reserve, which passed all too quickly for us. The weather was ideal all the time, and although our training was by no means neglected, we had ample time for sports and recreation. A very successful Divisional horse show was held, and among the special features provided for our entertainment during that rest period was an open air concert given by Harry Lauder in the beautiful grounds of the Chateau at Willeman. The opening event of the concert was a march past in mass of the thirteen pipe bands of the Division, who, as may well be imagined, produced enough music on that occasion to satisfy any Scotsman. Which reminds me that Harry Lauder's first words as he mounted the platform and looked round at the assembled thousands of the 15th Scottish Division were " Are there any Scotsmen here ? " He wanted General McCracken to give the whole Division a holiday next day to celebrate the occasion !

In the afternoons we frequently rode or walked to the neighbouring town of Auxi-le-Chateau, a very interesting and old fashioned provincial centre. Our main object in going there was to visit the town bath houses, but we usually finished up in one or other of the cafes, especially in one kept by a very charming French war widow, where we used to meet other officers of the Brigade and hold a sing-song.

As for the men, if not on duty they were given the afternoons to spend in their own way, and their recreation mostly took the form of football, though many went to Auxi or just pottered around the countryside. Wild boars seemed to be fairly plentiful in that district, judging by the number of their tracks to be seen on the fringes of the woods, but though I once saw a whole family of these animals in the Bois-de-Auxi we never managed to get a pot at one.

For all that we were having such a pleasant and comparatively restful time at Buire-au-Bois, hard training was the order of the day from early morning until the early afternoon, and we were not allowed to get slack. Besides the ordinary drill, of which the troops were always very much in need after a long spell in the line, the battalion on several occasions was marched to a special training ground some distance away, where for the whole day we joined with the rest of the Brigade in practising what was to us a new form of attack, in which far more importance was attached to aggressive rifle fire than had hitherto been the case. The main feature of this special training was that the attack was carried out in short sectional rushes covered by rapid rifle fire. Really it was nothing new ; it was almost precisely the mode of attack as laid down in the old pre-war text books on infantry training, and it is a thousand pities it had not been adhered to throughout. There is no doubt it was their high pitch of training in musketry, and especially in the use of rapid fire, that saved the original British army at Mons and in the open fighting early in the war, but later on, in the training of the new armies, the rifle was neglected in favour of bombs and other new weapons, which, however effective they may be in sedentary trench warfare, are of little or no use in more open fighting, or even in repelling an enemy attack. The rifle is and always will be the chief weapon of the infantry, but the drafts of newly raised troops that were sent over latterly could scarcely be got to use the rifle, which they seemed to look upon merely as something on which to stick a bayonet. Had it been otherwise, a very different story might be written of the big pushes on the Somme and at Arras.

CHAPTER XLV

The Ypres Front—1917

LIKE all good things, our long rest back in Army reserve in due course came to an end, and the 15th Division was transferred north to the Ypres front, where operations on a big scale were impending. About the middle of June we bade a regretful farewell to " Beery Boys " and marched to Frevent, where the battalion entrained for Poperinghe. I with two platoons of " C " Company and the battalion transport were left at Frevent to follow by a later train, which we shared with a field company of our Divisional Engineers. The time of waiting we passed bivouaced in the meadows outside the town, and I remember the day was so hot that many of the men divested themselves of their clothes and indulged in sun bathing, or in laving themselves in a little stream that flowed across the fields. Fortunately there was an estaminet at the crossroads nearby.

After a hot and wearisome train journey that seemed to be a succession of stops and long delays, we detrained in the middle of the night at Poperinghe and marched out to rejoin the rest of the battalion at Canada Camp, near the little hamlet of Brandhoek. The distance was not great, but the men were dog-tired, and it was their first experience of those atrocious Belgian streets and roads paved with rounded cobble-stones which provide a very precarious foothold for iron-shod army boots. Many a crash and much profanity was heard during that night march, as some heavily laden man measured his length on those greasy cobbles. However, on reaching Canada Camp we fell out and slept by the roadside until daylight came and we found our quarters.

The Arras sector had seemed to us very different from

the conditions we knew on the Somme, and here in the Ypres salient the conditions we discovered were again changed. The section of the front line taken over by the 15th Division lay some three or four thousand yards almost due east of Ypres, and to reach it we had to pass through the city and the famous Menin Gate, always a very shelly neighbourhood. The German positions ran in a wide half-circle along the rising ground to the east, including the St. Julien and Zonnebeke ridges, which although of no great height were of sufficient elevation to allow the enemy a field of view that commanded all the British trenches in the salient, as well as the city of Ypres and the country for some distance beyond. One thing that attracted our notice was that the whole countryside was covered by a mass of red poppies, growing even on the banks of the trenches where left undisturbed long enough.

Our own trenches in the low lying ground overlooked by the enemy were mostly very poor affairs, in fact, in some parts, owing to the waterlogged nature of the ground, the trenches were only three or four feet deep, supplemented by breastworks constructed of any old sort of material, which were easily destroyed by the enemy artillery and trench mortar fire. Dugouts there was none in those low lying trenches, the only cover being shallow cubby-holes cut in the side of the trench, or " elephant shelters " constructed of semi-circular sheets of corrugated iron covered by sandbags and earth. These provided very little protection from shellfire, but it is extraordinary the feeling of confidence any sort of shelter will give. I have seen a man, on hearing a shrapnel shell bursting overhead, cover his head with a newspaper.

However, in the five or six weeks we were there before the big offensive opened in the Ypres salient, we did not do a great deal of front line duty in the trenches; I think only three tours of a few days each. On the first occasion, I remember that the commanding officer with the company commanders, including myself, went forward to make a preliminary inspection of the trenches we were to take over. We started out on horseback very early in the morning, and on passing through Vlamertinghe we followed a path across the open fields that brought us to the northern outskirts of the city. There we left our horses behind a ruined house near " Salvation Corner," one of the most dangerous parts of Ypres, though we did not know that at the time. I have already mentioned the trouble we had with our horses when we took them under shellfire on a previous occasion at Arras, but it was nothing to what we found this time when we returned from our short visit to the front trenches. The mounted orderlies left in charge could scarcely hold the maddened beasts, and it was only with the greatest difficulty that I eventually succeeded in mounting my " charger," a great heavy coffin-headed brute that I think had pulled a coal-cart in his mufti days. Once I was on his back he immediately took the bit between his teeth and set out at a crazy gallop for home, regardless of all obstacles in the way. The flat fields in that part are intersected by numerous broad ditches, which had then been bridged by wooden gangways, and by sheer luck he took all these flimsy culverts in full career without disaster, thickly coated with mud and slippery as they were. We had gone a long way through Vlamertinghe with its greasy cobble-paved streets before he became blown and I managed to regain some control over him, and I think by that time I was in as big a sweat as he was !

A good deal of our time behind the lines at Ypres at this time was spent in continuing the new attack practices we had commenced before leaving the Arras sector, and here also special training areas were set aside for the use of the Division. To reach these areas usually meant a fairly long march, which in itself was good exercise for the troops, of the kind they really stood in need of then. The marching powers of our battalion at that time were poor because of the number of semi-crocks we had received in recent drafts, and I think the other battalions of the Division, and no doubt other divisions also, were in much the same state. However, we did what we could to get these new drafts into fit condition and fighting trim for the forthcoming offensive, but it was very evident that the recent operations at Arras had taken a heavy toll of our best personnel, especially in non-commissioned officers.

I remember early one morning while the battalion was on the march to the Divisional training area we were overtaken by the commanding officer, who instructed me to return to Battalion H.Q. for the purpose of conferring with the adjutant, Capt. Watson, in the preparation of a scheme for a trench raid on rather a big scale that was then intended. Watson and I sat over it most of the forenoon, but the day being warm, and perhaps feeling the urge for a little diversion, we adjourned to the back garden of the billet for a quiet game of badminton with a set that had been dug out from somewhere. We were hard at it with our tunics and shirts off, when the Colonel unexpectedly returned, and we had to listen to some plain talk on neglect of duty and wasting time on frivolities while a matter of the most serious importance was in hand, and so forth. For all that, we had already drawn up a raid plan and time table, which when actually carried out shortly afterwards proved a big success.

In addition to the ordinary battalion exercises at this time, special demonstrations for officers in the latest methods of attack (always attack and never defence) were held at the 5th Army School training ground back beyond St. Omer. We rather liked attending these demonstrations, because apart from the instruction we received at them, the journey gave us an opportunity of looking round the town of St. Omer, one of the most interesting old towns I have seen in France.

Although St. Omer is in France, there seems to be a large Flemish element in the population of that district, judging by the names over the shops, although I never heard Flemish spoken there. On the Belgian side of the frontier no great distance away, the prevalent language

N

is Flemish, which our Jocks soon discovered contains a
large number of words common to our own broad Scots
dialect. In that part of Belgium all public notices and
shop signs are in Flemish as well as French, and I remember that on the night of our first arrival at Poperinghe, as we marched out of the station, one of the first
signs that met our eyes was the word in huge letters
'' BREWEREI,'' the sight of which raised a joyous
cheer from the men. We shortly afterwards found that
the brewery had been converted into a bath house for
soldiers !

Towards the end of July, as preparations were nearing
completion for the big attack, which had for its main
objective the distant Passchendaele Ridge, I was instructed to report immediately at the War Office in
London, where I learnt that I was seconded to the
King's African Rifles for service in East Africa. I
cannot truthfully say I was sorry to get away from that
hell's kettle the Western Front ; no man in his right
senses could be ; but all the same I could not help feeling
mean at the thought of leaving the battalion just then;
knowing as I did what they would soon be going through.
Of all the officers who had served throughout in that
battalion since I first joined it in France, that is ex-
cluding non-combatants such as the Quartermaster and
the Transport Officer who did not go into the fighting
line, there were only three besides myself when I left.
Within a week I read in the official casualty lists that
two of them had been killed, and the other followed not
long after.

CHAPTER XLVI

I Go to East Africa

In August 1917 I sailed with a draft of officers and N.C.O.'s for East Africa on the Union Castle liner " Galway Castle." The voyage was uneventful, although two days after leaving Plymouth we passed early one morning through the track of a steamer that had been torpedoed during the night. When I say the track, I mean the floating debris of loose gear that still littered the surface of the sea, but we saw no enemy submarines nor any survivors from the sunk ship. The " Galway Castle " herself was torpedoed on the return trip that same voyage.

If I had felt mean two or three weeks before when I left the poor old 12th H.L.I. in Belgium cheerfully bracing themselves for that costly push against the Passchendaele Ridge, I experienced a recurrence of the feeling when I had time to look around and make the acquaintance of the other officers of the draft on board bound for the same destination as myself. A number of them certainly had real war service to their credit, but too many of that draft proved to be " trench dodgers " of the most flagrant kind, conscripts and men who had seen little or no service in the field, some of whom I think had now applied for service in East Africa in order to escape being drafted to a more lethal front. One or two of them actually boasted of how they had managed to " wangle " it ! It had never occurred to me before that a transfer to another front could be looked upon in that light. However, when conscription is in force I suppose an army must be made up of all kinds.

We travelled to East Africa by the Cape route, and as the " Galway Castle " took us only to Durban, where we were held up for nearly a fortnight awaiting a transport for the East African coast, it was five or six weeks altogether from the date of leaving home before we reached our final destination, Nairobi, the headquarters of the King's African Rifles. Despite the tedious waits at various ports up the eastern coast, the latter part of the voyage provided plenty of interest for me, as it was my first visit to these parts of Africa.

On the journey south we called at Ascension Island and St. Helena, the first of which is nothing but a gigantic slag-heap rising out of the ocean, containing only a large cable station and a lot of small goats. There is little of interest also at St. Helena, apart from the house occupied by Bonaparte in his exile there, although the " capital," Jamestown, a little one-eyed place of a single street running up a steep ravine, reminded me very much on a small scale of Sierra Leone, from where the negroes in St. Helena seem to have come originally.

Cape Town and Durban, however, are both fine cities, though very dissimilar in many ways. While the population of Cape Town contains a large Dutch element, Durban is predominantly British, but in both places we found the people very friendly and eager to do all they could to give us a good time during our stay. When we arrived at Cape Town, I remember all the hotel and public bars were closed while an Australian troopship remained in the harbour, some of the troops from her on the previous day having wrecked a public bar and started to paint the town red. The " Aussies " were not popular in Cape Town just then.

After our enforced stay of almost two weeks at Durban, where we spent a glorious time surf-bathing and generally loafing around in ideal weather, we continued our journey up the East African coast to Dar-es-Salaam, calling at one or two ports on the way. There we were again held up for some days owing to the lack of transport facilities, but at this place we were kept well employed instead of being allowed to loaf about at our leisure as at Durban. It was very hot, and I think some of the new officers

and N.C.O.s from home were not altogether enamoured
with their first experience of hard outdoors work in
tropical Africa.

But although we were kept busy during our stay in the
Detail Camp at Dar-es-Salaam, we still had ample time
to look around the town, the capital of the late German
colonial government and in which the German civilian
population were still carrying on their usual avocations
undisturbed by the British occupation. I was rather
surprised to find it such an up-to-date and well laid out
town, with some fine buildings and many large houses
of the tropical bungalow type along the neatly kept main
streets and in the European residential quarter, where
all the streets are shaded by rows of the gaudy red-
flowering " flamboyant " tree. It was strange at
first to see so many German civilians, including women
and children, moving freely about, and to be welcomed
into a cafe by a pink-faced close-cropped German pro-
prietor as if our countries were not still at war. I heard
that some of the German ladies in Dar-es-Salaam had
their own little feminine ways of carrying on the war for
their country, but the less said about that the better. It
was strictly forbidden to have anything to do with the
German civilian population, especially the women,
therefore these minor tragedies could not be officially
reported, although I believe they were known to the
military authorities.

Dar-es-Salaam at that time was full of troops of all
descriptions and of an amazing variety, including white
South Africans, black West and East Africans, Indians
of various nations, and even a battalion of Belgian native
troops from the Congo. These last I noticed by their
tribal marks belonged mostly to the Benguella tribe,
who have, or had, the reputation of being cannibals in
their own country. Dar-es-Salaam being then the headquarters of the Commander-in-Chief of the British forces
in East Africa (Gen. Van Deventer) the staff of course
was very much in evidence, and it must have been a very
large staff indeed to judge by the number of red-tabbed

field officers to be met with everywhere. They seemed mostly to be South Africans. Not even at an Army Headquarters in France had I ever seen so many red tabs and decorations.

Eventually, with some other officers and details for the King's African Rifles I was sent to join a transport ship lying at Zanzibar. We made the short sea journey across the straights, a distance of forty to fifty miles, in a small tug-launch named the '' Stork,'' and although it took only a few hours, the pitching and rolling of our little craft during that crossing seriously upset the digestion of almost everyone on board and made it seem like days.

After the usual few days' delay at Zanzibar (a most fascinating place) we sailed in a B.I. boat for Mombasa, from whence we entrained for Nairobi, our final destination. There, on reporting at the Staff Headquarters of the King's African Rifles, I was posted to the 2nd Regiment, and along with some others was sent out to the big K.A.R. Depot Camp at Mbagathi, about ten or twelve miles from Nairobi towards the foothills of the Ngong '' Mountains.''

The K.A.R. camp out on the fringe of the Athi Plains at Mbagathi (so named from a small stream in the locality, a tributary of the Athi River) was an extensive affair scattered over an area of more than a square mile ; it was really a collection of separate camps belonging to the depots or training battalions of the various regiments of the King's African Rifles. New officers and N.C.O.s from home, or from South Africa (whence many were being drawn at that time), were for some weeks after arrival posted to the camp for a course of training, and especially for the purpose of gaining some experience in the handling of the native African troops they were now serving with. In my own case native troops were not altogether new to me, as in those far off days at the beginning of the war when I was with the Nigerian Land Contingent we had often shared duties with the native troops of the Nigeria Regiment. The natives I was now serving with, however, were entirely different from those I had known on the other side of Africa, but they were equally good. In any case, Africans are always the same big children whatever part of Africa they hail from.

I should explain here that, although there had been a lot of big fighting in East Africa since the outbreak of war, the main German resistance had broken down shortly before the time I am now writing of, and of the dispersed enemy forces, all had surrendered or been rounded up with the exception of one small column that still kept the field under Colonel Von Lettow-Vorbeck. Our General Smuts, on handing over the command after the final defeat of the German main forces, had declared that the East African campaign was then practically ended, and that the work of clearing up could be entrusted to our native East African troops alone, that is, to the King's African Rifles. The large bodies of mixed troops we had seen at Dar-es-Salaam were at that time in process of being returned to their various home countries, or else transferred to other fronts.

Nevertheless, Colonel Von Lettow with his small force of experienced and hard-tried soldiers, European and native, held out doggedly in the field until news of the Armistice was received. In him the enemy had a leader they might well be proud of. For about fifteen months, with scarcely any supplies but the resources of the country (and what he captured from our Portuguese allies), he fought and evaded the several columns of King's African Rifles in the field against him; in Portuguese East Africa as well as the ex-German colony, and at one time before the end he even invaded Northern Rhodesia. What that long drawn out side campaign cost Britain I do not know, and whether it might have been ended long before the Armistice is not for me to say. Although throughout all that time there were only a few columns of King's African Rifles actually in the field against Von Lettow and his veteran die-hards, the coast ports of Dar-es-Salaam, Lindi, Kilwa, and many other centres far distant from the scene of the fighting, were up till the date of the Armistice, and for some time after, full of staff and administration officers, a very large percentage of whom were of field rank.

Another factor that perhaps mitigated against a quick conclusion being brought to that small but costly campaign was that few of the senior officers of the King's African Rifles themselves had seen service in France or on any other of the big fronts, with the result that whenever they had a brush with Von Lettow's forces and sustained forty or fifty casualties they seemed to imagine that one of the big battles of the war had just been fought, and that instead of immediately pressing the advantage gained, a breathing spell was necessary. I have heard that after the Armistice, Colonel Von Lettow-Vorbeck declared that on at least two occasions when hard pressed he was prepared to surrender, had the attack been immediately resumed, but on nothing further happening he again collected his forces and moved off to continue the game of hide-and-seek in the African wilds.

However, this digression has taken me a long way from Mbagathi, where I found myself stuck for most of the remainder of the war.

CHAPTER XLVII

TRAINING BLACK SOLDIER BOYS

DRAFTS of officers and native troops were sent from time to time from Mbagathi to the columns in the field, but I had not been there long before I was disappointed to learn that I was permanently posted to the Depot staff of the 2nd K.A.R. From then on for several months I was what is known as a " Depot Wallah," whose work was the training of recruits into soldiers fit for the field. We " Depot Barnacles " were very much looked down on by those officers returned from " the field," usually on account of sickness, perhaps after only a few weeks of active service there, and who may or may not have seen a few men killed and wounded.

As time went on and I became used to the new life, I began to find a great deal of interest in the duties at that training depot. The 2nd King's African Rifles to which I was attached belong to Nyasaland, as do also the 1st, these two regiments having originally formed the 1st and 2nd Central African Rifles before the amalgamation of the K.A.R. Our recruits were sent to us in batches from Nyasaland, and though they usually had been given some small preliminary training at the sub-depot there while awaiting a draft, they were still very crude material when they first came into our hands. But they were excellent material, being composed of raw Angoni, Nyanja, Awemba, Atonga, Yaos, and other tribes recruited in the wilds of Central Africa. None of them spoke a word of English, the common language understood by the great majority being Chinyanja, and their first lesson, if they had not been taught it already, was to repeat their own regimental number and also to recognise it when they saw it. I remember one recruit who used to inform us gravely that he was " Numba Sikisty-sikis-otty-otty " (No. 6600) !

It might not be thought that savages newly dragged from their native wilds (for I believe most of these recruits were furnished by their local chiefs in Nyasaland who received head-money for them from Government) would take readily to the white man's army life, but as a matter of fact, with few exceptions they learned very quickly and soon turned out excellent soldiers. It was not until their training had progressed to a fairly advanced stage that they were provided with boots and full equipment, but even in the early recruit stage, while they were still being put through elementary foot drill, they showed themselves so keen that sometimes after Taman (" Retreat ") parade in the evening, whole squads would turn out again of their own accord for the last hour of daylight to practise some drill or movement they had seen done by more advanced squads. There was keen rivalry among the various squads and platoons of these black boys ; they were natural sportsmen.

As for the native N.C.O.'s, who had all served for some years in the army, they were really splendid, and any one of them could give the correct command on parade as clearly and as well delivered as would be heard in the Brigade of Guards at home. All commands were of course given as usual in English, and they were quickly learnt and recognised by the recruits, who, as I have already mentioned, spoke no English. Apart from the actual executive words of command, all the training was carried out in the Swahili language, of which most of our Nyasaland askaris (soldiers) had a smattering, although the lingua-franca of their own country is Chinyanja.

It may be wondered how European officers not long out from home could be of much use in training fresh recruits in a native African language, but Swahili is not difficult, and we very soon picked up all the phrases necessary on the parade ground, including even the more technical terms required in the teaching of musketry. A knowledge of Swahili was compulsory in the K.A.R. for all officers and British sergeants, therefore having no option in the matter I used to fall asleep at night with a book on Kiswahili grammar still in my hand. I passed an official examination in the Swahili language, written and oral, within less than six months after my arrival in the country.

Each battalion of the King's African Rifles had its full complement of native N.C.O.'s and warrant officers, including a regimental sergeant-major, and as I said before they were all extraordinarily fine soldiers. In addition, and supplementary to the native complement, we had European sergeants and warrant officers, officially designated '' British Sergeants,'' though among them were a number of South African Dutchmen seconded from the S.A. forces for service with us. These Dutch N.C.O's were nearly all sent to us from the big South African army training centre at Potchefstroom in the Transvaal, and although with very few exceptions they were good men of the right kind for service in a native African regiment, there were among them a few Boers of the real unsophisticated '' back-veldt '' type, one or two of whom could not even speak English ! On two separate occasions I was sent to Nairobi to prepare the necessary summaries of evidence required in the application for a court-martial in the case of two of these '' British '' sergeants of my own regiment, and on both occasions I had to employ the services of another Dutch sergeant as interpreter. The charge in each case was issuing worthless cheques to tradesmen in Nairobi ; due I think more to sheer ignorance than any real intent to defraud (a chequebook was a new and wonderfully useful thing they had probably never heard of before !) and I am glad to say they both got off with a severe reprimand and some advice for their future guidance in these matters of finance.

Although, as I said, they were mostly all good men when one got to understand them, the ignorance and naivete of some of these South African Dutchmen whom the war dug out from the back veldts was well-nigh astounding at times. Some of them had fought against us in the Boer War, and I remember that in one draft from Potchefstroom there was one typical old " backveldter," Sgt. Oosterhuizen, who displayed on his chest the ribbons of the two South African war medals. In his attestation papers from the base I noticed his previous war service had been in the Orange Free State forces 1899/1901. On questioning him about it, he replied that he had fought at the Modder River and in other battles at which a newly made friend of his, Sgt. So-and-so of the Leicester Regiment, had also been present, and, although he had fought on the *other side*, he could not see why he should not be entitled to wear the same war ribbons as his friend ! We let him wear them.

CHAPTER XLVIII

LIFE ON THE ATHI PLAINS

IT would be tedious to describe in too much detail our life in that training camp on the edge of the vast Athi Plains, and although at times it seemed to us monotonous and too regular for those strenuous days of war, when even the United States had at last decided to join in the general cataclysm of warring nations, I suppose even we " depot wallahs " also were still doing our bit towards the common end in the way thought best for us by the " brasshats " at Nairobi. But often, especially when bad news reached us from the Western Front, I wished I was back there.

However, despite the monotony of the regular daily routine in the training of our bare-footed black soldiers, we had ample scope for recreation, and there was no excuse if we allowed ourselves to become bored with the life. It certainly was a healthy one, out all the time on those open plains at an altitude of over four thousand feet above sea level. Big game shooting we had in plenty. In prewar days I had often read books on big game hunting in East Africa, and also seen the advertisements on the same subject published by the B.E.A. Colonial Government before the war to attract tourists, but having myself spent so many years in other parts of Africa I was sceptical, and never believed that game still existed in such number as I saw on these great plains, and in the thinly wooded savannah country on the lower slopes of the nearby Ngong Hills. Of course we were on the fringe of the great southern game reserve, in which no shooting is permitted even with an ordinary game licence, but we did not bother much about that when we wanted meat or sport. It was said that game all over the country, even outside the reserves, had increased considerably during the war years, when of course the usual annual influx of wealthy tourist sportsmen was suspended.

The amount of game we shot was a mere flea-bite compared with the enormous numbers slaughtered every year by these licenced sportsmen. As a matter of fact, after the first novelty of it had worn off, which was usually very soon, we shot only for fresh meat. Often I have gone out with one of my South African friends and stalked various kinds of game with our field glasses only, without any thought of using our rifles if meat was not required. In any case, placed as we were then with very limited transport at our disposal, we had no means of preserving the heads, horns, skins and such like trophies so coveted by civilian sportsmen. We preferred studying the animals in their natural state, of which we had an unique opportunity, to leaving their carcases as food for the hyænas.

The Athi Plains and the surrounding country was, and perhaps still is, a perfect natural zoo at certain seasons of the year, especially just after the rains when the young grass is green and plentiful. Hartebeests (kongoni) and zebra were very common, and sometimes they used to be seen in mixed herds speckled over the plains as far as the eye could reach, like cattle in the fields at home ; each herd surrounded by alert outposts of the beautiful little Thompson's gazelle. Wandering independently in and about these herds were always a few dour-looking wildebeests (the " gnu " of the crossword puzzle), sometimes singly and sometimes in groups, though occasionally those quaint bristling antelopes would be seen in considerable herds of their own, especially towards evening when all the game were making for water. At these times I noticed that the wildebeests seemed always to take the lead in the long processions of antelope and zebra wending their leisurely way to water that often was several miles distant.

These hartebeests, zebra, and gazelle, and to a lesser extent the wildebeests, are what I might call the

" community " animals of social habits that we were
accustomed to see in numbers almost daily, but there
was a great variety of others that kept more to themselves, from the lordly eland and giraffe ; impala and
bushbuck ; buffalo and rhino, down to the bush pig and
hideous smelly wart-hog. All these (with the exception
of the wart-hog ; an animal that keeps to the muddy
banks of streams) we occasionally came across on the
plains, on which there is little vegetation but grass and
some scattered clumps of the flat-topped mimosa tree.
But in the stoney and wooded ravines or dongas cut
across the plains by the many small streams running to
the Athi River were to be found numbers of baboons, and
of course their natural enemy the leopard.

It is in the thickets in these dongas, I think, that the
lions lie up during the daytime, although most of their
hunting seems to be done out on the open plains at night.
The zebra, I was often told by settlers and natives, is the
lion's favourite prey, and wherever the zebra is plentiful,
as on the Athi Plains, there also are lions to be found.
They usually hunt in parties or families, and although
seldom seen unless beaten out from their lairs in the
thickets, they were frequently to be heard at their
hunting and love-making during the night. The distant
concert would usually be opened an hour or two after
nightfall by one lion, with what sounded like a few long
drawn out sighs or moans followed by a series of short
roars, but ultimately breaking into a crescendo of full-
pitched reverberating roars, that often would be taken
up by several other lions ; a terrific noise that carried a
long distance through the cold clear night air of these
upland plains. Sometimes the concert would break out
again just before dawn, the darkest and stillest hour of
the night.

Very early one morning when out on safari, through
my field glasses I once watched a lion (the only live one
I ever saw in Africa) making its way leisurely through a
scattered herd of zebra and antelope in the distance.
The herd appeared to go on feeding without any alarm,

though no doubt they would be keeping a very wary eye on their dangerous morning visitor ; perhaps they knew his lordship was just on his way home full-fed from a late banquet, and that there was nothing to fear from him for the time being.   In any case, I was often told by natives that zebra and similar game show little fear of lions during the daytime, apparently having full confidence in their own powers of flight when not taken by surprise.   In the ordinary way, a zebra in its prime can easily out-distance a lion, but sooner or later there comes a day when the zebra finds he cannot run quite so fast, and one night the lion gets him.   From that it would follow that every animal living in these wilds ultimately meets with a violent death, and even the lion himself, when decrepit old age finally forces him to seek out some quiet retreat in which to die, is in the end eaten by that filthy scavenger the hyæna, whose own remains in their turn are one day cleaned up by his cannibal kindred.

Hyænas were so plentiful as to be a regular nuisance around our camp at Mbagathi.   All night long their eerie mournful wailings were to be heard in every direction, and although said to be cowardly beasts, I know they can be very bold on occasion.   During the night one of these brutes actually entered the grass hut shared by me with another officer and stole the fresh skin of a fine grey baboon that had been shot the previous afternoon.   In that doorless little grass hut there was barely room to squeeze between our two camp beds, but that thief of a hyæna managed to get through and return with the skin from the inner part of the hut without awakening either of us !

Many of our askaris believed that the hyænas are not ordinary animals but ghouls (mfiti) who turn themselves into that form at night time for the purpose of feeding on corpses, and they had good reason for that uncanny belief.   When the Spanish 'flue epidemic broke out in 1918, the mortality among our native troops was fairly heavy, and the dead were buried in a cemetery we made on the wooded hillside not far from our camp.   It was only an unfenced glade in the woods, and bury the bodies as deep as we might, the hyænas invariably resurrected them before morning, leaving nothing but the unrolled red army blankets with the tops of skulls and the big thigh bones, the only parts of a corpse the hyæna is unable to devour. The ordinary cry of the hyæna is a dismal wail, but when excited or squabbling they break into a succession of yells and shrieks like maniacal laughter. Often during the night we heard peal upon peal of that unearthly laughter coming from the burial ground on the hillside, denoting that the " mfiti " were busy at their gruesome midnight feast. Whenever in the course of their training we took the native troops near to that hillside glade littered with glistening skulls, they always became silent and shook their heads with glances at one another.

o

CHAPTER XLIX

A " Cushy " War

At the beginning of April 1918 a new battalion of the King's African Rifles, the 4/2nd, was formed, of which I was appointed adjutant. This battalion was part of a new brigade of the K.A.R. then formed specially for overseas service out of Africa ; in Mesopotamia or Palestine it was rumoured, although at one time we heard we were intended for the Abyssinian frontier, where there had been a good deal of trouble since the beginning of the war. However, apparently we were not required after all, and I continued at Mbagathi until the Armistice put an end to the war on all fronts, although the business on the Abyssinian frontier (the " Mad Mullah ") took a little longer to clean up. I was disappointed that we did not go overseas, as I would have liked to see some service on one of the main fronts with those black troops whom we had trained up from the recruit stage. How they would have stood up to shellfire is a question, there having been practically no artillery in use in the long bush campaign in East Africa, but personally I think that, well-officered and with good British sergeants, they would have proved themselves equal to the best.

Our training in the new 4/2nd K.A.R. proceeded much as before, except that we were now a fully trained battalion ready for immediate service, the recruits being still in the hands of the Depot. With the other battalions of the Brigade we were frequently engaged in tactical exercises on rather a large scale, that often took us for long distances out on the plains or in the more broken and wooded country of the foothills. For that sham warfare blank ammunition was of course used, but sometimes in our make-believe battles the whine of a real live bullet would be heard, and once or twice there actually were casualties. That was because some of our askaris considered that it added to the interest and provided a little realism in these otherwise tame shows to mix a few rounds of live ammunition with the blank cartridges served out to them ! Consequently it was necessary to make a very close inspection for live ammunition, which probably had been purloined on the rifle range for this sporting purpose, before taking our native troops out for field manœuvres.

One of the duties that fell to the new battalion about that time was the furnishing of a special force consisting of two companies for the purpose of disarming and interning part of the 2/6th K.A.K., who for some time had been showing serious signs of insubordination and mutiny. The three battalions of the 6th King's African Rifles were raised during the war mostly from ex-German native soldiers captured in the field, who were given the choice of enlisting or going into a prisoners' internment camp. Needless to say, these three battalions composed to such a great extent of ex-enemy soldiers were not employed against the German forces remaining in the field, but were sent north on what was known as the Somali Patrol for service on the Abyssinian border. I should think that to preserve discipline in battalions recruited from that sort of material, a special type of British officer and N.C.O. would have been called for. However, because of the insubordination that had developed in its ranks it had been found necessary to return the battalion in question for disbandment or reorganisation, and the disarming of them was carried out at a place called Kiu on the Athi River about seventy miles south of Nairobi, the task being accomplished mainly by a stratagem and fortunately without bloodshed, although there might well have been a serious outbreak just then.

Another little local affair carried out by troops from Mbagathi before the Armistice was an expedition against the Parka tribe of Masai. As far as I could ever learn, their only offence was their refusal to furnish recruits for the Carrier Corps, but whatever the cause, the B.E.A. Government had apparently considered it necessary that they should be dealt with. Beyond pillaging a few '' dukkas '' belonging to Indian traders, I believe that throughout that little war the Masai made no attempt at any real aggression, or to raid the isolated shambas of the European settlers in their vicinity, although there seemed little to prevent them from doing so at the beginning before troops reached the district. Their attitude, I think, was mainly that they wished to be left alone. However, the punitive expedition, consisting of two companies with a section from the Machine Gun School, proceeded to the Parka Masai country near Lake Naivasha, where only one "battle" was fought, in which of course the Masai got very much the worst of it. These fantastic naked warriors, with their black ostrich feather head-dresses and big buffalo-hide shields painted red black and white in the heraldic design of their tribe, never had the slightest chance against trained troops armed with rifles and machine guns, though many of them fell dead in a plucky and desperate attempt to get to close quarters to use their great long-bladed stabbing spears. I don't think that expedition was much liked by the Imperial officers who took part in it, at any rate not by those who had seen fighting against a real civilised enemy armed with modern weapons.

The Masai, from what I saw of them, appear to be a very fine race of savages, the finest I think I have seen in Africa. In that I am referring to the genuine nomad Masai of the plains, and not to their contemptible Kikuyu and other imitators. Tall, and with a peculiar mongolian type of features, except that the nose is usually well formed, these Masai are utter savages, showing little or no inclination to adopt the white man's ways, and their whole interest in life seems to be centred in their cattle, of which they possess great herds. I have been told by settlers that it is almost impossible to obtain Masai boys for work on the shambas, except perhaps as cattle boys ; a congenial occupation for them. In their

own life they frequently move their villages or
'' nyamatas '' from place to place in search of fresh graz-
ing grounds for their herds, their wanderings taking them
over the great plains as far south as Mount Kilimanjaro.
But though they lead a more or less nomad life in the
finest game country in the world, they do not appear to
be hunters. I have seen Masai herds-boys watching their
cattle and apparently quite uninterested in antelope
feeding among the cattle within easy spear-throw of
them. With their hair plastered down with some oily
red substance into a pigtail, and pieces of white bamboo
stuck in a row into the upper part of each ear, they
ordinarily go about naked except for a profusion of brass
and copper ornaments and a small flap of skin or red
blanket slung over one shoulder. For the purpose of a
pocket to hold their tobacco or snuff and other little
necessities, they often use old tobacco tins or similar
receptacles stuck through the widely distended lobes of
their ears.

The Masai appear to have quite an elaborate military
organisation of their own, all the young men on reaching
a certain age being compelled to serve for some years as
'' elmoran '' or tribal warriors. During that time they
are not allowed to marry and are kept to a restricted diet
of milk and meat, the latter often being eaten raw and
in huge quantities. Besides raw flesh, they drink the
warm blood from living cattle before the beasts are
finally slaughtered. I could never quite understand the
enforced celibacy regulations for these young warriors,
in view of the fact that all the unmarried girls seem to
live with them in the same big communal huts ; but once
a girl is definitely married (by purchase) to some warrior
who has completed his military service, she has a hut of
her own, and there can be no more '' messing about with
the troops '' for her if she values her life.

CHAPTER L

END OF THE WAR—CLEARING UP

I HAVE mentioned how despondent we felt when bad news reached us from France in the early half of 1918, and how in those dark days I often wished I was back on the Western Front. As time went on and the situation in France improved, we eagerly followed the course of events, until one day we had the great news of the Armistice. The troops, officers and British N.C.O.'s as well as the native Africans, were of course jubilant at the prospect of an early return to their home countries, and I am afraid that for a day or two discipline was slack. For my own part, I must confess that when the news of the Armistice was officially confirmed and we knew that the war, that had come to seem almost the normal course of existence for us, was definitely over, I could not help feeling somewhat depressed at the thought of all those old comrades, who, less fortunate than myself, were then lying mouldering in the far-off battle-scarred fields of Picardy, Artois, and Flanders.

Orders were received for the immediate disbandment of all the service battalions of the King's African Rifles, and a few weeks after the Armistice we left Mbagathi for Nyasaland, the home country of the 2nd K.A.R. I will not attempt to describe in detail that long and dreary journey to Central Africa, except to say that owing to the lack of transport facilities it was a succession of tiresome delays, and that it took us about two months altogether to reach our destination. At one place, Lindi, a fever-stricken spot on the German East African coast, where we were held up for two or three weeks awaiting a transport, we picked up the whole of our 3rd Battalion, and by the time we reached Beira in Portuguese East Africa we had

a very large number of native troops under our charge
(well over two thousand, as far as I can remember),
with very few officers and white N.C.O.'s to assist us in
handling them. These latter had mostly become
redundant and gone home ; the few that remained with
us having volunteered specially for that duty.

From Beira we proceeded to Chinde, and from there,
by relays in the available river craft, up the Zambesi
River to Chindio, the starting point of the railway to
Nyasaland, where we entrained for our final destination,
which was the Depot camp at Lembe, a small village a
few miles from the town of Blantyre. On arrival at
Lembe at the conclusion of that long journey, which, as
may be imagined, entailed no small amount of work for
us in the handling and feeding of such a large number of
troops at a time when transport and other arrangements
were exceedingly difficult, we finally handed over to the
permanent staff of the Depot and became redundant ourselves.

I spent a few weeks in Nyasaland before leaving for
home, however, and in that time I had an opportunity
of seeing something of the country, which I found to be
very different from East Africa. Down on the lower
reaches of the Shire River where it joins the great
Zambesi, and also in the north where the country around
the shores of Lake Nyasa is very low lying and hot, I
should think Nyasaland is rather unhealthy, but up in the
Shire Highlands where I spent most of the time, the
climate is fine and well suited for permanent European
colonisation. In fact, during the rainy season while I
was there, it was quite cold, and the rain mists sweeping
across the heather clad hills in some parts reminded me
of Scotland. Blantyre and Zomba (the capital), the two
main towns in the Shire Highlands, are both thriving
little places with fairly large European populations and
up-to-date stores. The whole district seems to be
dominated in every direction by the huge rounded bulk
of Mount Mlanje, which is believed by the natives to be
the special home of the " mfiti "—the hyæna-ghouls !

Game is not plentiful in that upland part of Central Africa, however, though I was told there is plenty of shooting to be had in the lower lying country to the north, and in fact, one of our officers who accompanied a party of disbanded native troops to the Fort Jameson dlstirct in the Awemba country, succeeded in bagging a lioness and an elephant, besides a number of smaller game such as koodoo and other antelopes.

CHAPTER LI

SOUTH AFRICA

I LEFT Nyasaland in February 1919 in the company of some other officers bound for South Africa and the old country, and after the usual long delay at Beira in Portuguese East Africa, in this case of about a fortnight, which nevertheless we contrived to pass very pleasantly, we managed to obtain a passage in a transport to Durban, where again we were held up for a long while, and where again we put in a fairly good time. That second sojourn of mine in Durban, where I had already made a number of friends on my first visit, is in fact a happy memory.

Although the war had ended some months before, Durban seemed still to be full of men wearing military uniform, especially in the later part of the day after business hours. I think most of these youths must have donned uniform when the day's work in office or store was over, perhaps because uniforms were fashionable at that time and popular with the ladies. These soldiers for an evening seemed mostly to belong to obscure volunteer or cadet corps, and I noticed the majority of them sported a strange medal ribbon which I discovered was for the '' campaign '' some years before against the Zulus under the chief Dinizulu. If all the people I saw wearing that ribbon had actually taken part in the show it commemorated, it is no wonder the misguided Dinizulu had such a rough time. As a matter of fact, I learnt that the Dinizulu rebellion (it was nothing more) was quelled without much trouble by the police! However, the people of Durban, despite the craze then prevailing among the male sex for military fashions, gave us a very good time, and I hope some day I may have the opportunity of revisiting that delightful city on the southern Indian Ocean.

Eventually, one or two other Imperial officers and myself were given a passage from Durban on an old tramp steamer named the " Voronej," an ex-Russian boat chartered by Government to convey to their home country the last details of the West African troops still remaining down south. She was an ancient boat ; a most dreadful old tub, with an old fashioned bowsprit, and I think in her youth she must have served as a transport in arctic waters during the Crimean war, because her portholes were permanently closed and could not be made to open. A more unsuitable steamer for a voyage to West Africa it would be difficult to imagine. One could not walk from end to end of her without having to clamber up and down all sorts of upperworks, over a litter of loose deck gear. In any case, we did not do much walking at certain times of the day, because they used to kill pigs on the so-called promenade deck ; first scalding the poor brutes with boiling water and scraping the hair off them, before getting on with the actual killing part of the business !

This steamer the " Voronej " was filled chock-a-block with native West African troops, among whom I found more than one old acquaintance. It took us six days to make the voyage from Durban to Cape Town, and on arrival at the latter port we Imperial officers applied to the local military authorities to be taken off the old tramp and to be allowed to join a decent transport to our destination in the United Kingdom, instead of creeping up the West African coast in that old death trap. Our request was granted.

Very fortunately for us, during our stay of over a fortnight in Cape Town we were given quarters in the old Castle, instead of being sent up the hill to Fort Knocke or one of the other forts, as might have been the case. Immediately on landing we were put into five days quarantine because of the Spanish 'flue, Cape

Town, as we heard having suffered terribly from two separate epidemics of that mysterious disease. The quarantine as regards ourselves must have been a mere matter of form, however, for although we were confined to the castle precincts during the first five days, we had the free run of the place all the time, and we were allowed to join the officers' mess, in which, besides the officers of the battalion then garrisoning the Castle (the 7th S.A. Infantry ; better known as the Greenpoint Rifles), were the G.O.C. and his staff. We had a very good time while we lived there, and we could not have been better treated by the G.O.C. and staff or by the officers of the 7th S.A. Infantry, all of whom without exception were good fellows.

I think most visitors to Cape Town are unaware of the existence of that old Castle, nor for that matter do most of the inhabitants of Cape Town themselves appear to know much about the interesting relic they have in the very midst of their fine city. It is known as the " Castle," but one must not get the idea that it is a towering castellated building with turrets and all that sort of thing. It is no more than an old citadel ; a squat businesslike old fort built by the Dutch two centuries or more ago, with the arms of the Free States of Holland still carved in stone above the main entrance. Instead of being situated on the hillside above the town,where one might look for such defences, it is down by the water-side close by the fruit market. No guns nor any modern defences are mounted there now, the old castle being only a barracks and the official headquarters in Cape Town of the South African Command.

I mentioned that the 7th South African Infantry were in garrison at the Castle. Their men and officers appeared all to be Dutchmen, and in the mess the officers usually spoke in the Dutch language among themselves when we were not present. Then for our benefit they politely switched over to English, which all of them spoke as well as any Englishman. In conversation with these officers, I soon discovered that to a man they were keen nationalists, and that they did not seem to hold a very high opinion of British troops. That opinion no doubt was based on the experiences of the South African war, although none, or very few of them, evidently had seen any service themselves. However, we never argued with them on these subjects, because we could see that, apart from their dogmatic political ideas (and no Scotsman is more dogmatic or pig-headed than a Dutchman), they were a real good set of fellows. That red-hot nationalist obsession seems to be a characteristic of the South African Dutch, and yet in picture houses and elsewhere I have seen the entire assembly rise spontaneously to their feet on the playing of the British National Anthem, which is more than I saw in Glasgow and other towns on my arrival home.

The Dutch people in South Africa interested me greatly. In Durban the population is predominantly of British extraction, but in Cape Town it seemed to me the Dutch element prevailed. And yet it was very difficult at times to distinguish the one from the other, for the reason that · there are so-called Dutchmen bearing British names and vice versa, and they all appear to be bi-lingual, speaking Dutch and English indiscriminately. That of course is essential there nowadays ; both languages being officially recognised by the South African Government and therefore necessary for all government employees.

I think the South African Dutch, the " Taal " as they call it, must be an easy language for a Britisher to . acquire, especially a Scotsman. While we were quartered in the Castle they gave us for a batman a young Dutchman from the " back-veldt " who could not speak a word of English, but with what I had picked up from our " British sergeants " (from Potchefstroom) in the King's African Rifles, and by filling in the rest with good broad Scots, I managed very well to get over the language difficulty with that back-veldt youth. It was he who told me all about the Dinizulu rebellion I have already referred to.

CHAPTER LII

HOME—AND SOME REFLECTIONS

WE sailed from Cape Town in March on the Union Castle liner "Briton," which was crowded with civilian passengers now making a long deferred visit to the old country, and during that voyage I realised for the first time the wealth and prosperity the war had brought to many people. I saw much more of the same thing when I reached home, but that is a subject which has nothing to do with this narrative.

On arrival home I was given the usual period of leave allowed by the Colonial Office to officers seconded for service in their employ, and in the course of that leave I was taken to a military hospital in Glasgow with an attack of acute appendicitis from which I nearly died. After a week or two of convalescence they posted me to the 1st Battalion of my old regiment the Highland Light Infantry, then stationed at Aldershot, where I put in a spell of peace-time soldiering ; a monotonous and boring profession that I feel sure I could never endure for any length of time. The battalion was composed mainly of young lads recently recruited, and only in a few of the warrant officers and sergeants did I meet with any friends of the old war days.

*   *   *   *

Eventually I obtained my discharge from the army, and shortly afterwards I sailed back to that part of Africa from which I had come to join up in the Scots Guards, at what now seemed an immensely long time before. On that steamer I met many of my old friends and acquaintances, few of whom had done any war service, and I was immediately struck by the affluence of these "indispensables" who had stuck to their very profitable jobs throughout, and of whom some were now ostentatiously displaying their newly gained wealth in endeavouring to buy the special attention of the steamer stewards at the expense of those few passengers like myself who could not afford it. That galled at times, but never on reflection did I regret having gone through with the great adventure of my lifetime, and should the same set of circumstances ever arise, I think I would do the same thing again, and leave the wealth to those who think most of it.

The war that made such a tremendous break in the lives of those who went through it, gradually became a hazy and confused memory, and it soon appeared to have been completely forgotten by the others. But for a long time after my return to civilian life, my dreams were often filled with those memories, and sometimes I seemed to be talking and making the same old jokes with comrades long since dead, some of whose remains are perhaps now being turned up by the ploughman in the peaceful fields of France and Belgium.

*   *   *   *

As I said, the Great War has now receded into the dim horizon of the past, and every year it becomes a fainter memory. Quite recently I witnessed a parade of ex-Service men, and I was struck by the fact that the youngest of them there seemed to be approaching middle-age. But a younger generation that were infants at the time of the Great War has now grown to manhood, and that new generation will have a big say in the making of the next war.

I do not denounce war, nor do I believe it can always be avoided in the future ; there have been wars since the beginning of mankind, and I believe they will continue so long as human nature remains what it is. Nations after all are very like individuals ; with the same jealousies, and subject to the same moments of excitement and passion in which all regard for the consequences is thrown to the winds.

In this narrative, however, I have endeavoured to describe as accurately and fully as my memory, aided by my rough diaries, serve me, my own actual experiences in the Great War; the bright as well as the dark side, and if what I have written can give the younger generation some conception of what war really means my time will not have been wasted.

* * * *

Even now, after all these years, little incidents occasionally occur that bring home a vivid memory of the war to those old stagers who went through it, although perhaps quite meaningless to others. Not so long ago I read a newspaper report of a Police Court case in which a man was charged with disorderly conduct and creating a breach of the peace. His defence was that he had been a sergeant in the army during the war, and on going into a public house "some said 'Good Old Sergeant'!" And that was how the trouble started.

INDEX